If You Dare Tell...

Rick Joyce

ISBN 978-1-909121-38-6

www.acornindependentpress.com

ABOUT THE AUTHOR

Although the author has written many successful technical non-fiction books, this is his first biographical book

At 21, he was deeply affected by the discovery that his mother had been repeatedly sexually and physically abused as a child by his granddad. Suddenly he understood why his mother stared glumly into space for hours at a time and could be found sobbing uncontrollably for no apparent reason.

His mother's mental health deteriorated to the point where she spent a lot of her time in hospital and Rick held his Granddad directly responsible. He was determined to seek revenge and became obsessed with doing so. At his darkest moment, he came close to committing murder, but eventually he saw the violent man he had become and decided to change for the better. He sought treatment for his alcoholism and turned his life around.

His story is incredibly moving and inspirational.

ACKNOWLEDGEMENTS

The writing and completion of If You Dare Tell has only been possible due to the exceptional support from some very special people. In particular I would like to thank my publishers Leila and Ali for their professionalism and guidance. Other people who have played a significant part in the books completion in one-way and another include: Barbara, Harry, Lee, Mike, George, Anna, Atalia and Jane.

I would also like to thank all of the real people who are characterised in the book, especially my brothers and sister, my ex-wife and children, good friends and other family members, you know who you are!

I dedicate this book to my real nan

PART ONE:

HOW IT BEGAN

1

BORN IN SCANDAL

August 1941, World War II: England – like the rest of the world – was facing an uncertain future. Despite England's history as a powerful nation, people were very worried about their loved ones and what might become of them if the worst happened. Most of the men of fighting age were being drafted into the Army, Navy and Air Force, while women were taking many of the jobs that had previously been done only by the men.

Life went on as usual in many ways, and in Chigwell a little town outside central London, Grace arrived at a front door accompanied by her only confidante, Alice, her nan. They had come to complete the plan that had drained Grace's energy for the last seven months. How Grace could have kept the secret from all but one person for so long was extraordinary, even to her.

Mrs Edwards opened the door to find Grace crying in her nan's arms. Mrs Edwards knew at once that the girl was in labour.

'Fetch the doctor,' she said to her husband, 'and go and get Maisie for me – now.'

Mr Edwards understood that this was one of those occasions when he had to ask no questions and do as he was told. He would carry out the instructions to the letter.

Her own body had told her when it was time to put the plan into action and Grace had arrived at the house just in time. This was to be her first baby.

*

It was January when Grace first knew of her true condition. It was difficult enough for her parents to feed everyone in the house already, and she knew that announcing her pregnancy would not only bring shame on the family, but that it would add unwanted pressure. She knew she had to hatch a plan that would allow her to have the baby without anyone knowing. The father of the baby was not at all interested in meeting his responsibilities, so Grace planned very thoroughly for the day she would give birth.

The cold January weather was good for Grace, allowing her to hide her shape under layers of baggy second-hand clothes. She resolved to keep wearing them until it became unbearable. Fashionable clothing was not commonplace in East London at this time, and Grace could hide her condition well, so well in fact that nobody suspected a thing – well nobody but her nan. When Grace arrived for a regular visit, Alice decided to broach the subject.

'I've noticed you're looking a bit flushed these days, darling. Is there anything you want to share with me, or can I offer any advice?' She gave her granddaughter a knowing look, which had the desired effect.

Grace broke down in tears, fearing that she was going to be exposed.

'Oh, Nan, I'm scared! What have I done?'

Alice was a wise lady and lived alone. If anyone knew the gravity of the situation, Alice did. She had lived through World War I and she had seen it all. To help Grace now was very important to her, and if things went wrong, she too would be embroiled in a family scandal, so together they devised a plan.

Mr Edwards arrived back at the house with Maisie, and the doctor arrived ten minutes later. Grace was having contractions every five minutes now, and the doctor decided to prepare to deliver the baby in the house. Mrs Edwards, being a mother of four, and who had had two of her children born at home, was not put off by the situation in which she now found herself. There would be plenty of time to find out more about the girl in due course. Meanwhile, it was her duty to fulfil her role and help Alice, her old friend and neighbour.

The baby was born in that house on the twenty-fourth of August, and as with all successful births, any thoughts of scandal were soon forgotten when the little bundle was passed to Grace to hold. Grace knew she must not bond with the baby, and had prepared herself for this moment. She held the baby with tears rolling down her cheeks and stared into its pure and innocent face. She had not known whether it would be a boy or a girl, but had chosen names for both eventualities. The paperwork was filled in with the baby name 'Sally'. The space for the name and occupation of the father was left blank.

Part of the plan included the baby being taken away from Grace and given into the care of the organisation where Mrs Edwards worked, which looked after orphaned and unwanted babies. It was far from ideal, but so were the circumstances, and there was no other option. It was the hardest decision that she had ever had to make, and she knew it was going to be a long time before she could come to terms with it.

After two days convalescing, Grace went back to her grandmother's, where to everybody else's knowledge she had been staying for a couple of weeks. The plan had worked. Both Grace and Alice were, in some respects, proud of their achievement.

Mrs Edwards was a good friend to Alice and she had the necessary connections to ensure that the paperwork would leave no trace of where exactly the baby came from. Sally was in good hands, and the organisation was very good at placing orphaned children into foster homes and babies into families.

Six weeks passed, and little Sally was to be placed with a loving couple in Southend-on-Sea who had been married for six years but who were unable to have children. Avril and John collected Sally, and John was surprised by his wife's suggestion when they got home.

'John, I'd like to call our baby by a different name. She would feel more like my baby if I could rename her Rose.'

John liked the name Sally, but as he knew it was Avril who would be with the baby more than him, he reluctantly agreed.

'Okay dear, I don't mind, but we will have to tell her when she gets older what name she was given at birth, as it is on her birth certificate.'

Avril agreed, and so a loving bond began between them all. John's parents were overjoyed, and the family were set for a bright future.

But after three joyful months with his new family, John had to go back to the front line as an army motorcycle despatch rider in Merzig in Germany, where the English had successfully held back the German forces for several weeks. He came home from army duty only three times between the time Rose became his daughter and early 1944.

During that time, German troops had placed many land mines around the French town of Metz, close to the German border and striking one with his motorcycle, John was killed.

This proved to be a turning point in young Rose's life.

*

Rose adored Avril and everybody commented on Rose's smile and her bubbly personality. The love between them was evident and they enjoyed doing everything together, but things changed slightly after John's death. Avril took it as well as she could, but she was vulnerable and she let her guard down. The military policeman who delivered the heart-breaking news of John's death was well-positioned to exploit this and began to work his way into their lives. Avril was glad of the support and guidance of Hugh and within a year they were married. This seemingly insignificant event changed Rose's life for ever and even had an impact on the family that she would one day have.

Hugh soon became master of the house and wasted no time introducing his own rules and forms of discipline. Hugh abruptly stopped their regular visits to Violet and Joe, John's parents, and insisted she call him 'Father'.

'But, Hugh, they are Rose's grandparents,' Avril protested; but being of a timid nature it took very little effort for Hugh to silence her with aggression.

'Well, Avril, Rose will not be seeing them any more, and I do not want my word challenged ever again. Is that clear?'

The ferocity of Hugh's voice frightened Rose and she heard her mother whimper in reply.

The grandparents, however, would not give up and tried many times to see Rose. Every time Hugh would tell them that they did not have a granddaughter.

*

Within weeks, Hugh had killed Rose's lively personality. She grew more and more confused and unhappy as her four-year-old mind tried to make sense of the changes in her life. Whenever she cried, she would be locked in her room for days without food. Although Avril couldn't bare to see what was happening, she too was scared of Hugh. When she had protested, albeit very quietly, she was told in no uncertain terms that *he* was the master of the house. Rose started to lose the feeling of love that she had developed for Avril and thought that they both hated her.

Rose and Avril were forbidden any contact with other people, apart from the odd trip to Avril's mother. These visits were the only happy occasions for Rose. She would be dressed in new clothes and given treats.

Rose knew nothing of Christmas or birthdays or any celebrations at all until she started school. School was one thing Hugh couldn't take away from Rose. She delighted in getting her uniform and being out among other people brought out a confidence in Rose and her mother that had been long-suppressed.

Although he did not like to let Rose go to school, Hugh saw the potential it gave for further discipline. Acting the concerned father, he insisted Rose's teacher tell him about any misconduct.

He was a very convincing man, and his military police uniform commanded respect. Of course, Hugh gave Avril strict instructions about what Rose could and couldn't do after school. Homework must be done, and if there was no homework, then Avril was to set some of her own.

Rose was scared of her father and avoided him when she could, but he would often come into her room and tell her to sit on his knee while he asked her about what she had said and done at school. He stroked her hair and her legs, throughout these conversations. At first Rose thought her father had changed and that he was pleased with her at last, but his words weren't warm or reassuring. On Wednesdays, Rose would have to explain in detail about how she would change into her PE skirt with the other girls. Her innocent five year-old mind could not grasp why she was being asked such questions.

At the end of these strange conversations, Rose was warned not to tell anyone what was said, not even her mother. All she knew was that she had to do what he said.

It wasn't often that Rose did anything wrong, but somehow Hugh would manage to find reasons to reprimand her. He would start by sitting her on his knee and talking to her while stroking her hair and legs, and then turning the talk around and showing her the kind of discipline he would deal out. He would put her across his knee, lift her skirt, lower her knickers and smack her four of five times before asking her if she understood why she was being smacked.

Rose didn't understand why this was happening, but was too scared to say so. Over a period of a year or so, Rose had become used to these punishments to the point where she actually started to believe that she must have done lots of bad things to deserve it.

*

Rose soon found her bubbly self-confidence again and made friends. Her teacher was very impressed with her work and by the start of her second year at school, Rose had risen to the top of the class. Her teacher told Avril that she should be proud of her daughter.

Rose was popular, and had been invited to go around to her school friends' for tea on several occasions, but she knew it would make her father angry so she made excuses. However, she desperately wanted to play with her friends and after a good school report, she plucked up the courage to ask.

'Mum, would I be able to have a friend round for tea one day?'

'We'll have to ask your father, dear.'

Rose knew what the answer would be, and wished she had not asked. That evening, when her father arrived home, dinner was set and her mother began.

'Rose has something to ask you, don't you, Rose?'

A shiver went down Rose's spine and she wondered why she had ever thought she might be allowed.

'Come on, girl, spit it out,' her father said in a harsh and cold voice.

Avril had already asked Hugh before they sat at the table, and had been told that she knew the rules, but he wanted to hear it from Rose.

'Father,' Rose began nervously, 'may I have a friend to tea one day, please?'

The silence lasted about fifteen seconds, which seemed like an hour to Rose.

'What have I told you?' her father shouted. 'Get up to your room – now! I will be up to deal with you after dinner.'

Avril shook with fear and wanted to say something, but she knew it would be no use. Rose ran to her room with tears streaking down her face. She knew she wasn't allowed friends: this was at the top of the list of Father's rules. She knew those rules like the back of her hand, but her confidence had got the better of her. She knew that his regular visits to her room would now increase and she would suffer for what she had asked for.

Rose sat on her bed waiting to hear the footsteps on the stairs that would bring the pain she knew she would have to experience again. The sound of Hugh's hand slapping Rose's bare skin was one Avril had got used to, and the muffled cries sent a shiver down her own spine. She had first-hand experience of her husband's strength, and could not do anything for Rose on this awful day.

After twenty minutes she eventually heard Rose's bedroom door close as he left the room, and the heavy steps on the stairs made her sit up and start to clear the used dishes from the table.

2

IF YOU DARE TELL ANYONE...

Although Rose was withdrawn and very quiet at home, she was the opposite at school. She relished going to school in the morning and being around grown-ups who were kind to her, and who would compliment her on her achievements, no matter how small. Rose got on well with her classmates and never squabbled with them. She enjoyed her time at school so much that as soon as it got close to home time, her demeanour changed. Her teacher just assumed that she was tired, but mentioned Rose's low energy levels in the afternoon at a parents' open evening nonetheless. Little did she know that this would have severe repercussions.

Rose was nervous about what her teacher would say, but deep down she knew she would get a good report. Her face blanched when her teacher mentioned her energy levels, as she knew Hugh would punish her severely for this. Rose was not looking forward to getting home that evening; she could feel the atmosphere in the car, and she knew that her father would be working out what he would say and how he would turn Mrs Carter's comments into a reason for reprimanding her.

'Get up to your room now,' her father said as they entered the house. 'I will be up to deal with you after dinner.'

Rose knew that she would be going hungry that night and went to her room to await her fate.

'Please be gentle with her,' Rose's mother pleaded as she placed the dinner plate on the table, 'She has done well at school, and is top of her class. She's a good girl.'

'Hugh swung his arm around and caught Avril's face with the back of his hand, with force enough to send his wife crashing to the floor.

'Don't you tell me how to bring up my daughter!'

Hugh was now towering over his wife, who was curled up on the floor awaiting more of the blows that she had come to expect. Avril was five foot tall in her socks and weighed just eight stone. How could she ever fight back against a six foot man of fifteen stone?

Why do you think the girl is top of the class?' he ranted. 'It's because of me, not you.'

Avril couldn't concentrate on the words being shouted at her.

'If it was left to you, the girl would be bottom of the class, and we would have to deal with humiliation of having stupid child.'

Rose could hear her mother's screams and was petrified. She wanted to make sure her mother was okay, but she knew what would happen to her if she left her room – what was coming to her was already bad enough.

Then everything went quiet and she knew it wouldn't be long. After what seemed like an hour, she heard her father's heavy footsteps on the stairs and tried to hide under her bed sheets as if it would protect her from what was to come.

'Get out from under there – now!' her father bellowed.

'You know why I'm here, don't you?' he shouted, 'You've let me down girl, you've let yourself down, and you've let your teacher down.'

Rose crawled out from under her bed sheets, crouched on the edge of her bed and sobbed uncontrollably.

'Get your clothes off – now,' her father ordered in a low but harsh voice, 'I'm going to teach you a lesson.'

Rose removed her jumper, skirt and blouse as she had on many occasions before, expecting to be smacked, but was ordered to remove all of her clothes. Rose was now nine years old and this was a frightening prospect to her. Although she sometimes had to pull her knickers down to get smacked, she had never been ordered to remove *all* of her clothes before in front of him. She knew better than to protest and she did as she was told.

Rose could not understand the confusing mix of fear, humiliation and shame, as her father stared at her with hunger in his eyes.

'Now then,' her father said in a cold harsh voice as she stood in front of him, 'explain to me why you're lazy.'

Rose stood there not knowing what to say; whatever she said would be wrong.

'Come on, girl, speak! Has the cat got your tongue?'

Rose couldn't speak, even if she tried to, her sobbing affected both her thoughts and her breathing.

'You are going to stand there until you give me an answer,' her father said. She knew he was looking at her. She felt vulnerable and was now getting cold. She opened her eyes in an attempt to look at him and try to ask for his forgiveness, but this only triggered a reaction that she had not been ready for.

'What are you looking at, girl? Don't look at me, just think about why you're here.'

Rose quickly lowered her gaze, but in that brief moment she had seen that he was sitting back with his hand underneath a blanket that was on his lap. Rose was innocent, and could not have known what he was really doing.

After twenty minutes of standing there, her sobbing had subsided, and she knew she had to await her father's next instructions.

'Okay, come here, girl,' he said, pulling her across his knee, 'since you can't tell me why you've not been concentrating at school, I have no choice but to punish you.'

Rose knew what to expect now, and was in some ways happy, as it meant that it was nearly over. The repeated assault from Hugh's hand made her buttocks and the top of her legs red raw. Rose lost count of the number of smacks she had received. She was left sobbing and shaking with shock.

Such was the severity of her experience that she was visibly traumatised the next morning and was kept off school for two days until she had recovered. Although she did not receive any words of comfort or support, she knew that going back to school would cheer her up.

The atmosphere in the house reached an all-time low, and Rose was glad to be back at school.

One evening after dinner, just two weeks after her father had reprimanded her so violently, Rose was surprised by his offer to cheer her up.

'Rose, I have decided to treat you to a trip to the zoo, and if you want to, you can invite a friend to come, and she can also stay over.'

'Oh, Father, thank you so much!'

Rose was delighted but was too young to realise she was being manipulated. Even Avril was blind to Hugh's plan.

*

'Mother, look at the monkeys! Aren't they funny? Look at them looking at us.'

Rose and her friend were having a great time at the zoo; they had hot dogs, lemonade and ice cream, and were allowed to buy some souvenirs for their teacher.

'Okay, girls, come on. Let's get back to the car. It's time to go, now.'

Hugh had been a very different man on that day, and Avril wondered why he had been so kind. It was not in his nature, and she was curious about his reasons for such a change. She assumed that he felt guilty about the severe punishment.

The fun continued when they got home.

'Okay girls, you can take a drink and a snack up to the bedroom, but don't make too much noise.'

Rose and her friend sat on the bed and chatted about their day and what they enjoyed the most. They were giggling at how the monkeys scratched themselves and how the penguins waddled along. They mimicked the animals and were laughing out loud. For once the house felt like a normal, happy place to be.

At about 9:00pm, Hugh entered the room and told the girls that it was time they got ready for bed, and then left them to it.

The girls dutifully took off their clothes and put their nightdresses on. Little did they know that Hugh had drilled a small hole in the door many months earlier and was watching their every move.

When Avril had previously caught her husband peeping through the hole in the door, he had told her that he needed to make sure that Rose was doing as she was told.

Avril knew better than to question her husband. Despite her knowing full well why the hole was there, she did nothing about it. On one occasion, she had encouraged Rose to put up a poster on the other side of the door, but it was soon removed on the grounds that the drawing pins would damage the wood.

Hugh always insisted on putting Rose to bed as she grew older, and after closing her bedroom door it would be some time before he could be heard coming down the stairs. Avril grew increasingly worried about Hugh's behaviour, but she also knew that she could not voice her views.

*

School and home life continued in this way for Rose for the next couple of years, and while Rose enjoyed being able to have friends round to stay on a regular basis, she was always curious as to why she was not allowed to stay with her friends. She was still reprimanded on the odd occasion despite not deserving it, and she accepted the smacks that she got from her father as part of her life.

When Rose reached the age of eleven, she was allowed out more often but not beyond their street, and she had to be in much earlier than her friends. Despite this, she had a great time with her neighbours and relished the freedom of being away from the oppressive atmosphere of her house.

'Oh, mother I'm sorry for being late, but I didn't mean it; my watch has stopped.'

Being ten minutes late started a chain of events that were going to have an impact on her life forever.

'I'm sorry, love but you know I'm going to have to tell your father. If he finds out that you were late in without me telling him, you know what he'll do, don't you.'

Avril was so afraid of her husband that she dreaded what he'd do to her if he found out she had not told him.

Rose pleaded with her mother not to tell him, and she was crying when Hugh walked in the door.

'What's going on here?' he asked.

'It's Rose,' her mother whimpered. 'She was ten minutes late coming in, and I was getting worried, so I told her off.'

Avril looked at her husband and saw his half-smile drop and a frown form on his face.

'There's no need for you to do anything. I have already told her off, and she is going to bed now without dinner.'

Avril really didn't want her husband to do anything, and was hoping that she had said enough to avoid things escalating.

'*I'm* the one who decides on what punishment should be given!' he roared.

Rose ran to her room and Hugh ate his dinner in total silence, glaring at his wife.

Rose was hiding under the sheets when her father came in.

'Okay, girl, get out from under those sheets now, and take off your clothes!' There was something very different from anything she had heard in her father's tone. Standing there before him naked and frightened, she wondered why she wasn't crying.

Her father placed his hand on her hip and started talking to her in a calm voice.

'Come here, girl,' he said softly. 'You're getting too old now for me to be smacking you like a child. I want to be able to talk to you so we can work things out.'

Rose was getting nervous, and could not understand why she had had to remove her clothes.

'You are a young lady now, and I am not going to smack you any more; but how am I going to get you to understand when you do things wrong?'

He had both hands on her hips now, and drew her towards him.

'You are my daughter, and I care about you, that's all.' He bent down to kiss her small and undeveloped breasts and Rose shuddered. 'Don't move or say anything, just listen to me.' He towered over her and ran his hands around her body, while telling her that he was going to be kind to her from now on, in the hope that she behaved. He placed her on the bed and Rose tried to switch off while he penetrated her eleven year-old body.

After telling her things that just washed over her, and doing new things to her, he eventually stopped and adjusted his own clothing. It was the worst twenty minutes that she had ever had to endure, but she knew better than to complain. Rose was in severe pain, and although she knew that grown-ups made love in order to have babies, she also knew that what she had just had to endure had had nothing to do with love or having babies.

'If you dare tell anyone about this I will beat you so badly, you'll regret you ever thought of crossing me,' he said before leaving the room.

As much as Rose wanted to tell someone what had happened, she thought it would be futile and couldn't risk things getting even worse.

As soon as he left the room, Rose put her nightdress back on, got into bed and cried herself to sleep. She knew that what he had just done was completely wrong and wondered why she had deserved such an unhappy life. The most important thing was to make sure what had happened that night never happened again, and that depended on her being a model pupil and daughter.

*

It wasn't long before the bedroom "talks" from her father were becoming a regular affair, and the level of his abuse became far more painful and mentally destroying than Rose could have imagined. She was also ordered to do things to her father that went completely beyond anything she could have ever envisaged, and when she tried to tell her mother about what was happening, she was accused of lying and told that she had dreamt it. What's more, she was told that if she ever spoke of these things to anyone, she would be accused of being a witch and burnt at the stake or locked up in a children's home.

Rose had read stories about witches and believed that what was happening to her was as a result of her own behaviour. She was told that what she had to endure at the hands of her father was because she was a bad girl, and that her life would only get better if she did as she was told.

Rose was sure that what was happening to her was wrong, but was it? Who could she ask? She had to believe what she was being told, after all they *were* her parents.

Avril felt very guilty about not being able to support Rose, such was her fear of her husband. Deep down, she knew that Rose was telling the truth, but she didn't dare confront Hugh. She felt that she should tell someone herself but the fear was too great. Avril had become so brainwashed by Hugh's manipulating ways and knew that she had to tell him that Rose had spoken to her.

When her father found out that she had spoken out, the abuse became more severe and more regular. Rose had to develop a way of dealing with her father's attentions and just closed herself off mentally and emotionally, although she was still expected to put on a happy face in front of others.

Rose had been told at the age of thirteen that she had been adopted at six weeks old and that her real family were wicked. She had been told that she had been taken from them to save her from being sent to a home for unwanted children.

Rose believed what she had been told, and despite her unhappiness and hatred for the man she knew as father she had to put on an act of the loving daughter as and when he required. She was scared of him and he knew it.

Living in a house where she was now hardly ever allowed to bring her friends, or have any hobbies or any of her own pets, Rose felt very much alone. The only thing that she was allowed to do was to attend competitions with her father where budgies and canaries would be shown and judged.

Rose's role would be to show the birds, and as far as all were concerned she had bred them and was an expert bird breeder.

Rose was a beautiful young girl, and on these occasions she would be dressed in the best clothes and her hair would have pigtails with red bows.

It was obvious that Rose's youth and beauty had helped to sway the judge's decision-making, and it was not by accident. Hugh was a master at manipulation, and was a long-term committee member of the bird club. In reality Rose was not allowed to feed the birds or even enter the large aviaries that her father had built.

He spent many hours with the birds, and out of all of the medals rosettes and certificates that were awarded, none of them were in Rose's room even though some of them had her name on them.

Her father would display them in the living room, and would ensure that everybody knew that it was he who bred the birds. On the occasions when he attended the bird club he would take the most recent trophies and photographs, but Rose was never allowed to attend, and in truth she was glad not to be asked.

At the age of sixteen, Rose was a regular visitor to the local library, and instead of reading up on geography, history and religion as she normally did, she started to read up on law, and in particular child abuse. Her confidence was growing, and although her father still gave her regular disciplinary visits, she knew that it was only her actions that could end it.

She had been planning to do something wrong, in order to entice her father into her room. She knew he would be relaxed and not expecting trouble. He was shocked to the bone when she told him that she was going to tell her friend's mother about what he was doing to her.

Rose knew that this was a dangerous move, but she had thought it through. She knew that he would not hit her now, as he hadn't hit her for a few years. His new form of punishment had changed him completely, and she hated him more than ever.

Hugh knew that he couldn't start shouting and ranting, as his wife was in the kitchen, and the mood in the house had been good for too long for him to suddenly change things. He thought about what Rose had told him.

'Rose, I know I've not been the perfect father, but I've only tried to bring you up to be good and respectful to your elders.' He was worried now, and knew that his actions over the past five years were beyond anything that he could talk his way out of 'I think you've learnt your lessons now and I have made you the person you are.' He was clutching at straws. 'I think you know that I love you, as a father, and it's now time for you to start your adult life. The rules are over now you're an adult. I will do anything I can to help you.'

When Hugh was confident that he had dissuaded her from saying anything, he left the room without touching her as was usual.

To Hugh this was an end to it, although Rose was not sure if her plan had worked. Over the next few weeks and months she was surprised to find that she was allowed to attend dance halls and other social events that she had never been allowed to go to before.

Rose did not tell her mother about the discussion she had had with her father, and Avril was just pleased that the house started to take on a new and welcoming atmosphere.

Rose never let on to anyone about what she had had to suffer in the past and was glad that her threat alone had worked, as she wasn't sure she could have actually brought herself to tell a soul about the horrors she had endured.

3

HOPE

On a visit to a dance hall, Rose met a handsome young man.

'Hello would you like a dance?' he said as he approached Rose.

Rose was shy around men and naturally sceptical, but there was something in his voice that reassured her.

'My name's Pat Joyce – what's yours?'

'My name's Rose.'

'Shall we dance?'

Rose had good reason to be suspicious of men, but from the moment they were on the dance floor, she felt something she had never felt before. Despite her reservations, she could not stop thinking about Pat after they had arranged to meet again and said their goodbyes. She couldn't understand what anyone would see in her. Rose knew that her body had been abused, and this played on her mind. She told herself that she was not pure, and despite things having been out of her control she had always understood, from her religious education classes at school, that becoming man and wife meant that both should be pure, and for this reason she had never entertained thoughts of boyfriends or marriage.

It was hard for Rose to accept that she was not pure because of the vile actions of her father, but wanted to put it behind her. Her new-found freedom allowed her to meet Pat quite often and before too long he would arrange to pick her up and drop her off after going to the cinema or a dance hall. Her life was beginning to change in such a way that her torrid and awful childhood started to became a distant past.

Pat lived at home with his family, and it was not easy for him and Rose to spend intimate time together, but they eventually became lovers, and Rose felt real love for the first time in her life when they spent a night together at Pat's brother's house. She had never experienced that kind of passion, and although she didn't know it Pat had never fallen in love with anyone except her. For the first time in both their lives, they knew that they had met their soul mate.

Rose's new life was now emerging, and she glimpsed hope for the future while distancing herself from her foul secrets, which for the time being needed to remain hidden.

*

Rose was finding it more and more difficult to keep her grip on her bedroom windowsill, and, unable to find a foothold in the stems of the creeper on the side of the house, she decided that her only option was to jump. She held her breath, pushed out with her hands and feet and let go, landing squarely on the flat roof below.

With her heart pounding and her ears expecting the sound of her parents' voices any moment, she was surprised that all she could hear was the rustling of the leaves.

She expected to see the light from the upstairs hallway shining through her bedroom window as her father opened her bedroom door. The fear that she had been used to feeling some months before had reached a new intensity, but she fought the desire to cry. The night remained silent around her, although now she could hear the muffled sounds of her parents' angry voices from the living room downstairs.

'It's your only chance,' she said again to herself, gritting her teeth as she worked out how she was going to get to the ground without making too much noise.

Fortunately for Rose, there was a ladder already leaning up against the gutter. She climbed down it and made her way through the quite streets to see Pat. She knew everything would be okay if she could get to him.

That day had been one of the worst of her life. In her sixteen years she thought she knew what misery was, but her despair had reached new depths as she witnessed her one chance of happiness

recede before her eyes. Rose thought that everything her mother and father had said about her was true. She was a harlot – a useless, ungrateful and selfish waste of everybody's efforts. She didn't deserve to be happy. But despite what they had said, she dared to hope that the opportunity that had presented itself had not come to her by mistake.

All she had ever wanted was the opportunity to love and be loved, to be valued and trusted. She now saw it all slipping away out of reach – rightly so, she knew, but she was desperate enough to stretch out and try to grasp for the vision of love and security that had been held so tantalisinglybefore her.

Earlier that evening, Rose had stood sideways before the mirror in her bedroom, running her hand over the flatness of her stomach and examining her profile out of the corner of her eye. She analysed who she looked like; whether the soft dark auburn hair and her bright hazel eyes came from her real mother's side, or her small, well-proportioned nose had been a legacy from her real father?

She had a beautiful complexion, but had never been complimented on it by her parents, and she was unused to studying herself in such detail – a reluctance born in part from anxiety about what she might read in her reflection – but today was different.

Today it was not vanity that drove her to the mirror, but rather the need to discover who she was. She turned her head and saw her reflection smiling back at her, the bright, but empty smile that she had learned to adopt when anyone else was present.

A tiny, almost inaudible sigh escaped her lips as her gaze moved to her hand, placed gently on her stomach. She remembered reading somewhere that the stomach is the body's 'second brain', and certainly she had come to trust the familiar fluttered warning she felt in it now. But this wasn't quite the same feeling she got when she was afraid, or the one she felt when there was reason to be alert and ready to face whatever was going to happen next.

With the mirror forgotten, Rose took a step backwards and sat on the edge of her bed. She wondered whether this feeling could be excitement. But that didn't makes sense: the last few days had been some of the worst of her life, and had culminated in today, a

day of humiliation and the rage of her parents that had only just fallen short of a physical attack by her father.

Over just a few years she had experienced much more horror than many people do in a lifetime, but she had learned to control her emotions with a steely determination and was able to switch off at the worst moments. However, even her powerful survival instinct had been tested to its limits today.

She closed her eyes and could see again the expression on her mother's face as the doctor told them the news. Well practised in the art of withdrawing from her surroundings and letting the voices wash over her in a series of unconnected sounds, Rose recognized the disapproval in the coldness of the doctor's tone when he spoke to her, and the impatient sympathy in his conversation with her mother.

'Well, you'll need some time to discuss things,' he had said to Avril as he stood up behind his desk, barely able to disguise his relief that they would soon be going.

'I must say, Mrs Harris, Rose is very lucky to have a mother who's so patient and caring. Most girls in her situation could expect to see quite a different response from their parents – and would deserve it, too, some might say.'

Rose glared at the patronising doctor.

'Don't leave the decision too long. The sooner it's made, the better for all concerned.'

Rose fixed her eyes on the drab flower pattern on the carpet, which she felt reflected the characterless personality of the doctor himself.

With her eyes still downcast, Rose followed her mother across the room to the door. Pausing with her hand on the doorknob, her mother turned to look at the doctor with an expression of long-suffering resignation.

'Thank you, doctor,' she whimpered. 'You've been very kind, I'm sure. It's far more than the girl deserves.'

Avril sounded as though she was a caring mother who always had her daughter's interests at heart, but the reality was very different. 'I can't imagine what her father's going to say. He'll be so angry, what with all he's done for her education and everything. It'll break his heart, I know.'

Hugh had manipulated Avril for so many years that she had unwittingly become his puppet. Although she knew what he had done to Rose over the years, she could not bring herself to tell the truth.

Rose had difficulty keeping pace with her mother on the silent walk home, thankful for even this opportunity to postpone the moment of reckoning just a little longer. As they walked, she tried to concentrate on blocking out the thoughts that dominated her mind, as she repeated to herself with increasing desperation, 'It will be all right. It will be all right.'

As they neared the house, and Rose came ever closer to whatever lay in store for her. Her footsteps slowed, and it was only the occasional venomous glare directed at her over her mother's shoulder that forced her onwards.

Rose felt sick with relief when they found the house empty, and she felt that at least someone was looking down on her. As a bailiff, whose much-enjoyed job it was to evict hapless families from their council houses when they fell behind with their rent, her father often had to work unsocial and unpredictable hours, and Rose felt a fleeting pity for the poor people he was no doubt bullying out of their home.

She was sent to her room to await his return, a punishment her mother knew only too well would be far more effective than any she could inflict herself. As Rose was left alone to imagine the scenes, she tried to visualize her father's reaction, hoping to prepare herself by imagining the worst. But even her vivid imagination, which had been developed through years of experiences that were beyond most people's worst nightmares, could not prepare her for what was to take place an hour or so later.

After hearing her father's car pull up, she strained to listen to her parents' conversation, but was unable to make out what they were saying. The conversation carried on through dinner, and her anxiety mounted to almost unbearable proportions by the time she heard him coming up the stairs.

Crouching at the head of her bed she was trembling with fear and holding her breath while she waited for the door to open and the blows to reign down. Her father raged poisonous words about her being a whore and a prostitute that no one would ever want. Although he had been on the verge of hitting her several times during his tirade, he had drawn back at the last moment, fist raised above her cowering body, with what appeared to have been a Herculean effort of will. But somehow the things he had shouted at her hurt far more than the blows she had expected, and the coldness in his eyes had crushed the last traces of self-esteem from her already damaged soul. When he had finally left her room, and her broken-hearted sobbing had at last begun to subside, she had remained, crouched and despairing, on her bed, trying to think what to do next.

Whichever way she looked at it, things simply couldn't get worse, and her need to see Pat had never been greater. So there was little more to be lost by escaping through what she had come to know as her 'emergency exit' and going in search of him. Her parents were right, of course, and Pat would only be disgusted by her dishevelled and forlorn state.

She knew that she had changed overnight from the pretty, bubbly girl he had apparently fallen for into a millstone that no young man would want to be burdened with. But despite the force of her father's anger, she could not suppress the small voice deep in her mind that kept repeating the words she so desperately wanted to hear. *'He'll care. He loves you,'* it told her. She knew only too well what disappointment was, how futile hope was, but she knew too that she couldn't live without seeing Pat one last time, and couldn't bear to miss out on the chance, however slim it might be, that he would put his powerful arms around her and tell her that everything would be all right.

'Come in, Rose, come in. Pat is chopping some firewood in the garden; he'll be in shortly. Would you like a cup of tea?'

Rose was not used to such a kind and gentle voice, and this triggered the outburst of tears and emotion that Rose had been trying to hold together. She expected it to happen when she had Pat's arms wrapped around her.

'Come, come, Rose, things will be all right.' With her mother's intuition she knew instinctively what was wrong. She had been in exactly the same situation when she was a girl and had experienced the terrifying panic that Rose was clearly going through. She put her arms around Rose and whispered, 'You have a family here as well as at home, now, and we'll stand by you. All Rose could do was nod and sniffle. 'I'll call Pat and put the kettle on.'

Pat came in quickly, with a basket of chopped wood to put by the fire, and he could see in Rose's face that something was very wrong; he could also see by the look on his mother's face that she knew why Rose was there.

'Take Rose into the front room. I'll bring a fresh pot of tea, and we'll work out what to do next.'

Pat knew that there was something seriously wrong and he led Rose into the front room. Although he was nearly twenty-two years old and had gained considerable confidence from his experience in the Army, he knew that he would need to rely on his mother's wisdom and support more than he ever had before.

Rose sat down opposite and fought to find the right words. As stressed as she was, she felt safe beside Pat.

'Pat...' Rose started as she looked into his eyes, 'I know you are going to hate me for this but I have to tell you...I've been to the doctor today. I missed my last period.'

Rose held her head in her hands and sobbed, but instead of Pat moving away from her as she had expected, he leaned forward and put his arms around her. Despite his shock, he instantly knew there was only one thing he could do.

'Oh Rose, why would I hate you for that?' said Pat softly. 'We will get through this and be together.'

Pat's Mum came in with the fresh pot of tea. She sat down at the table and poured three cups before saying a word.

'Now then, the first thing we need to do is to meet with your parents and plan where you will both live when the baby comes along.'

Pat had not to say a word, as this was a moment he was glad to have decisions made for him, despite the fact that he was a confident young man and used to being in control. He was apprehensive, but happy in the knowledge that he loved Rose, and he knew that Rose loved him. Pat knew he had been irresponsible in getting Rose pregnant, but in the eight months that he and Rose had been together they had fallen in love, and they had talked about the long term. He was in no doubt about what he had to do. He now had the support of his mother, and it would not be long now before he would have the support of his large and loving family.

Rose knew that she would have to go back and face her parents, but she wouldn't be alone. For the first time in her life, there were people who really cared for her.

'Let me do the talking,' Pat told her. 'I want your parents to know that I am going to do the right thing and that your honour and future is my priority.'

Pat had only ever met Rose's parents twice before, and he was always curious about why she had not seemed to want him to spend any time at her house. He sensed that her relationship with her parents was not particularly close, as she never really spoke about them, but he had never pried.

On the way back to the house, Pat offered nothing but support and loving words. Rose felt overwhelmed by the love and kindness both Pat and his mother had shown her. She began to sob uncontrollably, not because of what she was about to face, but because the living nightmare of her childhood had come to an end.

The house looked cold and uninviting as they approached the door, and the small sound of twigs and gravel underfoot sounded like thunder in Rose's head. She tried to calm down, and held onto Pat's arm as if it her life depended on it.

Avril was visibly shocked when she answered the door. She was lost for words and the spiteful tirade that Rose expected never came, instead Avril called for Hugh to come quickly.

Hugh was taller than Pat by about six inches and of a bigger build, and being a step down only exaggerated the difference for Pat.

Before anything was said, Pat decided that he needed to take control. He had spent two years as a national serviceman with the Royal Artillery, which had given him confidence and maturity beyond his years.

'Mr Harris, can we please come in and discuss things? I need to assure you that I love Rose and I am going to do the right thing.' Pat had assumed that despite this being a very difficult situation for everyone, common sense would prevail and things would be sorted out amicably. He had no reason to think otherwise. Little did he know that Hugh was a hard, cold and callous man who was used to being in full control of those around him.

'Get up to your room now, girl!' he bellowed in Rose's face. 'And as for you, if I ever see you around here again you will regret the day your mother gave birth to you!'

With a controlled but nervous voice Pat tried to reason with Hugh, without success. Rose was still clinging to Pat's arm, and Pat had his hand on her to reassure her that he was not going to be bullied by Hugh.

Hugh stepped out of the doorway to grab Rose's arm as if to force her in, but Pat took a step back, taking Rose with him. He was strong and had no difficulty in moving Rose out of harm's way.

'Mr Harris, I've come round to assure you that I love Rose and that we both want your support,' Pat said with a controlled, but raised voice. 'I can understand why you are angry and upset.'

Little did Pat know the deeper reasons why Hugh was so upset, or, to be more precise, worried about what Rose had told him.

For the first time in his life, Hugh was in a position where someone was prepared to stand up to him, and he was not sure how to deal with it. His usual approach would have been to intimidate with his authority, or with the Alsatian dog that was normally by his side.

He knew he was going to have to yield to Pat's confident stance.

They all went into the dining room. The atmosphere in the house was unbearable to Rose. It was left to the men to discuss things.

'Mr Harris, first I want to apologise , but most of all I want you to trust me; I am going to meet my responsibilities and make Rose happy.'

Hugh was more interested in where and when they had first met and how many times they had had sexual intercourse.

This confused Pat. Why was his focus on the detail of what had happened and where it happened and not on the future for Rose? He was not prepared to give in to the interrogation, but assured Hugh he would marry Rose and give her anything that she needed.

He arranged to see Rose the next day, and assured her that until they had their own place he would spend all of his spare time with her.

'You're going to be a mother,' he reminded her, 'and your parents need to get used to the idea.'

Rose sat at the table staring down at her feet. As Pat's car drove off she knew that she would not receive any words of comfort or support from her parents, and used her well-practiced skills of switching off before the hateful words and verbal aggression began.

'You are just like your mother,' were some of the hateful words that Rose heard, and, 'that's why your family did not want you.' But these words did not really sink in, as she had long since learned to numb her emotions to avoid the pain.

Rose had never really thought about why she had been adopted. She had many friends who had been adopted because of the war, and she had assumed that that was the reason.

'I always knew you were a whore.'

She just sat and let the torrent of hateful words and accusations wash over her and thought about how lucky she was to have Pat.

Now it was confirmed. He did love her; he stood up to the person who had dominated her every day and action since she could remember.

Rose wanted to tell Pat the truth about her parents one day, but how and when was something she had to plan in great detail. Pat was a true gentleman, but she didn't know how he would react when she told him that her mother and father had been so cruel to her, and that her own life had been so lonely. This could wait, as she knew that she would be seeing him everyday from now on, and that no one could hurt her anymore.

For the first time since she could remember, Rose slept all night, and was up and dressed an hour before she was due to be collected to travel to the small college that she now attended. Rose was very well educated, and despite being articulate and worldly, she instinctively hid the awful truth that had been her life until now. From a very early age she had been warned not to form friendships, visit anyone's house alone or join any clubs. Only she and her parents knew the reasons why, but even when she was older and had friends, the consequences of telling anyone were, to her, spine-chilling.

4

THEIR FIRST HOME

'Please don't do anything, love,' Rose pleaded with Pat as he threatened to go round and kill Hugh. 'I have only ever had my parents in my life, and although my mother wasn't there for me all the time, her hands were tied, and I'd hate to lose contact with her now. I have *you* now, Pat,' she told him, 'and as soon as we can find somewhere to live I will leave home and be with you. We will be happy together.'

Pat managed to control his anger and emotions, he could not believe what had been going on. Rose eventually managed to convince Pat that she was no longer in danger from her father's attentions and that his priority was finding somewhere for them to live.

'Let's go to the registry office tomorrow and book our wedding, Rose. I can't stand the thought of you being there under his roof a minute longer than you have to.'

*

The following day it was arranged and they would be married on 6th May 1958, which was in just a few weeks' time. Pat had the support of his whole family, and between them they had helped to raise sufficient funds for a deposit on a rented flat and enough to cover the wedding costs. He was a hard worker and although he was working for a local builder, he took on his own private jobs for a bit of extra money. He was an all-round builder, and like his father and older brother William, he could lay bricks and undertake carpentry work with ease. His jovial character soon helped his popularity to grow, and work was coming in thick and fast.

Things were put in place so that on the day they were married they would move into a one-bedroom first floor flat in the seaside town where they lived in Essex.

Pat had a love for the sea ever since he came to Southend-on-Sea as an evacuee from East London in 1942. When he was sixteen he managed to get a job working on a local fishing boat and he knew that his own children would enjoy the opportunities that living by the sea offered.

Rose was surprised that her parents did not show any of the further signs of disapproval and although they were not supportive, and disagreed with many of the details of the arrangements, they allowed her and Pat to get on with things.

Had she known what Pat had done a few days after learning about her father's behaviour over the years, Rose would have understood why.

*

'Hello 57689,' Hugh said as he answered the phone,

'Hello Hugh, it's Pat here. I wonder if we could possibly meet up, as I'd like to discuss the wedding plans with you.'

Pat had promised not to 'rock the boat' as far as her parents were concerned, but he knew he had the upper hand, and wanted to make their wedding a day to remember for the right reasons.

'Could we meet in the park by the old church tomorrow at five o'clock?'

'Sure, Pat. I have a few ideas for the wedding that I think Rose would like.' Hugh was fairly sure Rose hadn't told Pat their dark secret and was keen to establish himself as a caring father in Pat's eyes.

'Don't tell Rose or Avril we are going to meet,' said Pat, 'as I want to arrange a nice surprise for Rose.' Pat was very convincing, and Hugh was pleased to be asked to contribute to the wedding in any way he could.

'Okay, Hugh, I'll see you tomorrow.'

Pat arrived early and, as it was raining, he made his way to a sheltered seating area.

The park was empty apart from two people walking their dogs some way off.

'Hello Hugh, over here!' Pat shouted as he saw Hugh enter through the park gate.

Hugh made his way over to the shelter, and as he approached Pat he had a big smile on his face.

'Well, Pat, you must be getting excited about the wedding,' he said in a friendly voice as he entered the shelter. 'Avril and me are pleased you're going to do the right thing by Rose and show that you are an honourable man.'

'Yes, that's right, Hugh; you are absolutely correct. Honourable man, that's me.' Pat's voice was coarse, and he was staring Hugh in the face with a piercing look in his eyes.

Pat began his well-rehearsed lines. 'You talk about "honourable" – you don't know the meaning of the word. I want to talk about the bad things you have done to Rose.'

Pat had planned for every eventuality, and was not surprised when Hugh protested his innocence while turning to walk away. Pat grabbed him by the arm and forced him up against the wall of the shelter with one hand at his throat.

'You're not going anywhere, mate!' Pat was ready for a fight, but had a feeling that it would not happen. He knew that the man in front of him was a coward, and he knew exactly what to say.

'I have decided not to contact the police, although I have spoken to my friend's Dad, who is a senior police officer, and he is prepared to look into things if I want him to.' Pat was bluffing, but he knew that Hugh would think very carefully before challenging his word.

Still pinned up against the wall, Hugh's face was going red as Pat applied more pressure. Hugh was visibly shaken at Pat's strength and confidence.

'Now then, Hugh,' Pat continued, 'you will not tell anyone about our meeting, especially Rose.' Pat was looking Hugh directly in the eyes, and could see the fear he had evoked in him. 'You will make an excuse for not being able to attend our wedding, and even if Rose seems disappointed, which I very much doubt, you will just tell her that you can't make it.'

Hugh was struggling for breath now, but he knew that Pat was too strong and agile for him to try anything.

'If you make Rose's life difficult in any way between now and when she moves out, I am going to kill you.' Pat meant what he was saying, and Hugh knew it.

'I don't want you to offer any help to us; it is not expected or wanted,' Pat continued. 'Why Rose ever decided to remain in your house is beyond me, but I guess she had no choice then, but now she has.'

Pat could feel Hugh's body shaking, and much as he wanted to avenge his future wife's honour and unleash the full force of his anger against the pathetic coward standing before him, he managed to control himself.

'Lastly Hugh, do not *ever* come to our flat; and if we do come to see Avril from time to time with the baby, make yourself scarce. Are we both clear?'

Hugh was numb with fear and shock, and as Pat released his grip, he mumbled his acknowledgement and slumped down on the floor.

Pat walked off, and knew that he had delivered his message with much more dread than he had envisaged.

*

The next few weeks were filled with excitement for Rose. She expected to wake up at some point and find out it had all been a dream, but she knew it was real and the wedding day was approaching fast. Her parents were being surprisingly quiet, although her mother was helping her with her wedding plans as much as she could.

'Unfortunately, Rose, your father won't be able to attend the wedding, as he can't get the time off,' Avril announced a few days before the wedding.

'Oh, that's a shame, Mum,' Rose said, secretly pleased at this news. 'Not to worry; you can take some cake back for him, can't you?'

The wedding was a simple affair, with a family gathering afterwards at Pat's family home. Pat's brother William was best man, and Tony, a long-term friend, was the only witness apart from the official clerk.

Rose had never seen all of Pat's family together and she was overwhelmed by the welcome she received back at the house. There were about forty people, and they were all paying her compliments and welcoming her into the family. Rose felt like a princess; this was truly the best day of her life.

The baby bump didn't really show at this point, but everyone knew she was pregnant. Rose felt she would be able to rely on some good advice from her new sisters-in-law when the time to have the baby came closer.

The happy couple moved into the flat that night, which had been prepared for them by Pat's brothers and sisters. They had clubbed together, and with the money that Pat had earned by working longer hours and weekends as a self-employed bricklayer, the flat was fitted out with a mixture of new and used furniture, pots and pans and everything that the couple needed.

Rose's new and exciting life had begun; for the first time in her life she felt free. Her mature attitude soon helped her to settle and begin the preparations for being a mum and housewife.

She had never even been allowed to cook a meal, but these things came naturally to her and the young couple were happy.

Rose now felt free of her father's oppression and was able to do something that she had wanted to do for a long time. She told Pat about her grandparents, Violet and Joe, who she had not seen since she was three and a half. Although she could remember them only vaguely, she was keen to get in touch.

Violet and Joe were overjoyed when they turned up at the door, and could not believe that their granddaughter was going to have a baby. Rose vowed to see them as often as she could, despite the distance she had to travel, which was only eight miles, but difficult for Rose by public transport.

Rose kept to her word, and Pat was only too happy to drive her there every month or so. She wanted them to enjoy their great-grandchildren and for her children to get to know them.

Rose's company was also always welcome with Pat's family. She was articulate and fashionable, and always had a smile on her face. Pat's mother was always ready to offer advice on matters of children, cooking or any other responsibilities of being a wife and mother. Rose didn't really need much help, as these things came naturally to her; but she knew that Pat's mum enjoyed giving advice, and readily accepted it. She also enjoyed just being part of the family.

Pat's brothers and sisters looked forward to the couple's visits, as they all had young families of their own, and quite often the whole family would gather for a party. It was a very close family, and Pat's mum enjoyed seeing all of her grandchildren together, which only happened on rare occasions such as weddings and christenings. These family gatherings were a stark contrast to anything Rose had experienced. She had no aunts, uncles or cousins, so it was extremely exciting to her, and feeling part of it all was to her, a wonderful feeling.

*

November soon arrived, and baby Elizabeth was born. Rose and Pat couldn't wait to show off their bundle of joy to friends and family. Life was perfect as far as they were concerned, even though the flat was small and rather cramped.

Storage was an issue and when Pat's drum kit fell off the wardrobe onto the floor, Rose almost dropped her newborn baby who she was about to place in the cot.

Pat ran into the room to see what had happened. Despite Elizabeth's cries they looked at each other and, as there had been no injuries, they burst into laughter.

Pat knew he would have to think about moving into a bigger place at some point, but for now the drums had to go.

Rose had taken to motherhood and being a housewife like a duck to water, and loved every moment of being with her baby and Pat. She wanted to try for another baby as soon as she was fit enough. Her reasoning was that having children close together would be good as they would be able to play together as they got older. Pat had no problems with her suggestion, and knew that he had the determination and work ethic to provide for his family.

It was no surprise then that Rose announced in April 1959 that she was pregnant again, and Pat was delighted with the news. They made enquiries to apply for a council house, and by the end of summer, having fulfilled the criteria, the family were made a priority. In September, shortly before the baby was born, they were given the keys to their first council house. Excitement filled the air for them both.

For Rose it meant not having to live in cramped conditions, although she had never complained about it, and she would be able to hang the washing in the garden instead of all around the flat. For Pat it meant he could expand his growing building business, as he would be able to build a shed to store his tools and equipment. Life was getting better for the family.

When they moved into their new house, Pat was keen to make use of the garden and decided to surprise Rose.

'I'm going to build an aviary for you so you can breed some birds,' Pat said as they were chatting over dinner one evening.

Rose's face turned white. 'No, love, I really don't think it's a good idea,' she said in a panic. 'I don't think I will have time to look after them, and I'd rather have something for the kids.'

'Okay love, but just let me know if you change your mind,' Pat replied.

On the few occasions when he had been at her parents' house he had noticed photos of Rose with rosettes, standing in front of her father's aviary, but he had never been able to encourage her to talk about them.

Pat was curious, and decided uncharacteristically to try and find out more about why she was so against the idea of his building an aviary. After all, the kids would enjoy it, surely. Once Rose had explained the history behind the photographs he understood exactly, and vowed never to mention budgies, canaries or aviaries ever again.

5

GRANDDAD'S TRUE COLOURS

I was born in November 1959, just ten days after my sister Elizabeth's first birthday. My mum thought she was having a girl, as her pregnancy was just the same as with Elizabeth, so they were surprised and overjoyed that I was a boy. The only trouble was that they hadn't thought of any boys' names. After three days they decided to give me part of my dad's name – he was Patrick and I was Rick.

Our council house was cold during the winter months. Dad would often have to scrape the ice off the inside of our single glazed windows, but the open fire in the living room was rarely without coal or logs

Dad's work in the building trade allowed him to bring off-cuts of wood home regularly, and living next door to a coalman meant that we always had bags of cheap coal in the garden.

Mum had lots of friends in the neighbourhood and all the children would play together in the park or sometimes have picnics on the green. Mum knew how to stop us getting board and we'd have fun with Dad every weekend.

We visited lots of people but whenever we were at Nan and Granddad's Mum wouldn't let us out of her site. It seemed unfair that she wouldn't let Granddad take us to the park, but she knew how devious and manipulative he could be. The visits were always short. We would be dropped off and picked up by Dad. We had never really asked why he never came into the house; we just assumed he was

busy doing other things. Dad knew that Granddad was still not to be trusted, but he had to please Mum. It was a fine balancing act, and one he thought he was in control of.

*

One day Granddad suggested a trip to the zoo with the whole family. Mum and Dad both said no, but we nagged for weeks until eventually they agreed. When the exciting day finally came, I couldn't understand why Mum wasn't happier. Dad was also on his guard, and he never let us out of his sight. Despite this, Elizabeth and I had a great time.

On a visit to Nan and Granddad's house one Sunday morning, Mum happened to mention that Dad was struggling to find work, despite his best efforts.

'Rose, ask Pat if he would like to do some work for me. I'd rather give the money to him than anyone else.' Granddad knew that Dad wasn't keen on him and wanted to be on better terms.

'I'm not sure that's a good idea.'

'Nonsense. You need the money and I need someone to board up some windows and doors. I'm sure Pat would be able to do it and there could be plenty more of it to come,' Granddad said handing Mum some money and a bit of paper. 'Here's an advance to get the materials. Tell Pat to meet me at this address at nine o'clock tomorrow morning.' Granddad gave Mum a slip of paper with some scribbled notes on.

When Dad arrived at the road, he saw a police car and lots of activity about fifty yards ahead. On arrival at the spot it became apparent that the focus of activity was the house where he was supposed to board up the windows and doors.

Dad parked his truck and made his way over to speak to Granddad, who was standing with his Alsatian, talking to a policeman,

'What's happening here, Hugh?' Dad asked.

'Oh, hi, Pat. We are just about to evict a family who haven't paid their rent. I'm just about to serve them with the notice.'

Dad had actually worked out what was going on as he pulled up, but needed Granddad to confirm it.

'So what happens next, then?' Dad asked.

'We will serve the notice and then put all of the furniture and belongings in the front garden, and then you can get to work.'

Dad was fuming. Granddad had not explained why he needed the windows and doors boarded up and as Dad looked at the house, he could see two children staring out of the window who appeared to be about the same age as Elizabeth and me.

'Hugh, I would rather starve than have anything to do with this. Don't ever ask me again to do any work for you, and I am keeping the wood as compensation for you wasting my time.'

Granddad was taken aback and tried to persuade Dad to stay.

'This just goes to show how much you know me, Hugh, and it also confirms that you still have no self-respect or pride.'

Dad drove home and, after telling Mum about the incident, he went into the garden and built a shed with the wood that he had bought for the job.

Mum was really upset, and felt guilty about talking him into doing the work. She had no idea about the eviction, but she was not surprised either. She knew more than anyone how heartless and uncompassionate Granddad could be. That day, Mum told me that we wouldn't be able to visit Nan and Granddad for a while. The way she said it left no room for pleading or nagging to see their dog.

Seeing what happened to tenants who couldn't pay their rent served to motivate Dad even more to find work, and it wasn't long before he got a job with a house builder as a bricklayer. He was used to being his own boss and finding his own work, and didn't want to work for a builder, but he knew there was no choice.

Things worked out well, and the builder soon made Dad head foreman, which increased his pay considerably. Dad was a born leader and could manage men easily. He was also good at reading plans and dealing with architects and the local authority. He was an asset and it showed.

Mum did some work at home. She assembled electronic parts for a factory, which suited her as the parts were delivered and collected and it meant she could contribute to the family finances. Mum would get me and Elizabeth involved and we would help her pack the finished items in the boxes that were provided.

*

By 1964 Elizabeth and I were five and six and were attending the local school. Mum missed having us around and asked us if we'd like to have another brother or sister. We thought that would be great, and so did Dad.

In June 1965 our brother John was born. Mum loved motherhood, and while she did have some reservations about how we would take to the new arrival, there was no need of it, as her skills as a mother were so good that we were soon helping Mum with nursing John.

Mum knew all the tricks in the book, and had us bonded in no time. We were fascinated how Mum would have to express her milk into a bottle when she produced too much, and she involved us in everything to do with John. Elizabeth and myself would look forward to going to and from school, so we would help to push the pram, and Mum would always ensure that we kissed John before we went in to the school.

The teachers picked up on our enthusiasm and would get us to draw pictures of our little brother. Christmas's, Easter, birthdays and anniversaries were celebrated with good cheer and with other family members. It was important for Mum and Dad to capture these times with photographs, and they soon developed a huge collection of us all enjoying ourselves.

We were really happy and, despite the normal sibling rivalry from time to time, harmony prevailed in the house.

6

AN ADVENTURE

We were a huge and close family who loved to share time together. At least once a year we would all get together for a camping trip to Wales, Devon or Cornwall. It would not be unusual for a convoy of six or seven cars to head down to the West Country for a two-week camping extravaganza. When we set up camp it would include volleyball nets, goalposts, washing lines and all manner of improvised contraptions to make living in a tent for two weeks much easier.

Depending on where we camped, days out would typically include visits to the beach, mountains or moors. Wherever we went, whether it was raining or sunny, we enjoyed every moment.

Photos of the camping trips were fixed into the individual family albums, and when we all got together, we had a lot of pleasure in reminiscing about the holidays we shared together.

Dad raised the idea with Mum of an adventurous camping holiday somewhere exotic, but he wasn't sure it would be her cup of tea.

'Oh Pat that would be wonderful, the kids will love it,' she said excitedly as she gave Dad a hug.

All Mum ever wanted to do was to give us the childhood that she never had and for us all to be able to look back at happy memories and family photos – neither of which she ever had.

'We're going on a real holiday,' Dad announced at dinner after a visit to his sister, Victoria.

He explained that we would be going to Spain, and as Aunty Victoria had been there the year before, she would organise the trip. Aunty Victoria was Dad's second eldest sister and was great fun to be around. We would often go over to her house for a big family dinner.

She was a great cook and would bake beautiful apple pies using apples she had picked from the trees in her garden.

Plans were put into action, and they decided that July 1966 would be the date for a three-week trip. Dad worked hard to save up, and invested in a reliable car that was big enough to cater for all of us and all the camping equipment that we would need.

*

In February 1966 Mum suspected that she might be pregnant again; and as it was unplanned she was very nervous about telling us. Mum was sure that Dad wouldn't have a problem with her being pregnant, but she was worried about upsetting the holiday plans.

'Oh, Rose, that's fantastic!' Dad didn't even think about the timing. 'When is it due, do you think?'

'Well, I'd say it will be towards the end of September or beginning of October. I'm sorry, love; I know it's going to mess the holiday plans up.'

Dad could see the concern in Mum's eyes, and straight away put them to rest.

'Don't be so daft. Why would it be a problem? We are going in July, and we'll plan for all eventualities.'

Mum felt a weight lifted from her. Dad took the news in his stride with his usual confident manner, and was already thinking about what he would need to plan. It wasn't long before Dad had books and maps to plot the hospitals and clinics that were along our planned route.

Dad even learned some essential Spanish, and in a short space of time was proficient in the language. He said that it was important that people could understand him in case we got in any trouble.

*

As July approached, all preparations were made for the trip, and Elizabeth, our cousins and I were counting down the days on our calendars. Dad had been teaching us a few Spanish words, and we could often be heard practising them in our bedrooms and giggling.

Finally the day came to leave, and we set off on our epic journey at 7:00am as planned. Aunty Victoria, uncle Jimmy and our three cousins led the way in their car. The drive to the ferry port at Dover passed quickly and, as was usual on long car journeys, Dad kept us occupied by playing 'I spy' and other games. When we got bored with the games, Dad would have us all singing songs together. Mum sat in the back seat and tended to John, who was now thirteen months old, and, despite the many hours spent in the car, there were very few complaints from any of us.

By mid-morning we were on board the ferry and making our way to Calais.

The ferry trip was a welcome break, and we were treated to a visit to the captain's bridge by one of the crew. There we found very smart men in white uniforms and caps with gold braiding.

'How fast does the ship go?' I asked inquisitively.

'Oh, I think you'd have trouble keeping up with us on your pushbike, young man,' said the officer. He had been asked this question many times, and knew not to confuse children by explaining knots.

Dad and Victoria had planned the trip with military precision and had worked out where we would need to stop in order to erect the tents for the night. Aunty Victoria was older than Dad and was a born leader, which is why uncle Jimmy didn't get too involved in the plans. He did what he was told.

By four o'clock we had made our way to the first campsite. We played nearby while Dad and uncle Jimmy put up the tents and Mum and Aunty Victoria prepared the food.

By five thirty we were sitting around the fold-up tables and chairs enjoying a freshly cooked dinner. After all the pots and pans were washed up and packed away, Dad gathered all of us children around and had us singing songs while he played his guitar.

It was a typically warm summer evening, and by about eight o'clock we were getting tired. Mum prepared the sleeping bags and had us bedded down for the night by about eight thirty. Mum and Dad could now relax, and they sat at the table with my aunty and uncle drinking wine while they looked at the maps and discussed the next leg of the journey.

The next morning, we packed up and made our way to Paris. We were really excited. Dad had shown us pictures of the Eiffel Tower and the Arc de Triomphe before we left England.

'Okay kids, we are getting near Paris now, so look out for the Eiffel Tower and the Arc de Triomphe. There's a prize for the first one to see it.'

Dad knew we would see it at about the same time, and therefore we would both win.

'There it is, Dad! I can see the Eiffel Tower!' shouted Elizabeth in Dad's ear, and almost instantly I also shouted, 'I can see it, Dad!'

'I saw it first,' Elizabeth said instantly, but Dad was ready for this and interjected, 'You both saw it at the same time, so you both win,' But Elizabeth knew that she had seen it first, and tried to convince him of it.

'I think you *may* have seen it first; but it was close, so you both win.'

Elizabeth was happy with that, and no more was said. I wasn't bothered either way, as I knew that I was in for a prize.

We managed to park very close to the Eiffel Tower, and there was a buzz of excitement in the car. The smells of different kinds of food, coffee, tobacco and car fumes permeated the air, as we made our way to one of the many cafés where Dad and Jimmy ordered coffee and cakes and soft drinks for us kids.

The language we could hear being spoken amused us, and Dad noticed that I was staring at a couple sitting at the next table who were deep in conversation. Despite finding it quite funny, he had to tell me not to stare, but that was impossible.

Mum was very surprised at how well John was coping with the journey, and she and Dad had very few reasons for telling us off. We were obviously very excited about being on holiday, but on the odd occasion when we did misbehave, Dad's voice was enough for us to do as we were told.

He never smacked us, but if we were naughty we lost our privileges, such as being allowed sweets or were sent to our rooms. He told us that he didn't want to have to tell us off, but from an early age we knew he would carry out his actions to the letter.

After we had eaten, we made our way to the Eiffel Tower, and were surprised at how big it was.

Being a builder by trade, Dad was interested in architecture and was hard to impress, but even he was still staggered by the size of the Eiffel Tower.

Standing directly below and looking up through the middle of the structure was something that he had dreamed of. Dad then had an idea; he talked us into lying on the ground to look up through the structure while he took a photo of us. He was always taking photographs, and was determined to capture as much of this trip on film as possible. Uncle Jimmy had brought his cine camera, and was filming the holiday whenever he could.

We were soon up on the third level of the Eiffel Tower looking over the city of Paris. Uncle Jimmy filmed the whole trip up the tower, and had made sure to get plenty of shots of our looks of terror as the lift went up.

Elizabeth and I clung tightly to Dad. We were slightly nervous as we walked over the chequered plate and on looking down we could see the people on the ground, who looked like ants to us.

Although we enjoyed going up the tower, we were glad to get back down to ground level where Mum and Aunty Victoria were sitting on a bench enjoying the scenes. They had put John on a blanket on the floor, and he was playing with one of his toys.

'Hi, love,' said Dad as he approached Mum. 'That was exhilarating.

I'm so glad we decided to stop here. You wait until I get the photos developed!' Mum was really happy to see how excited we all were, our happiness meant a lot to her.

The next part of the journey was uneventful, and after one scheduled stop for fuel and to stretch our legs, we arrived at the campsite. Dad and Jimmy had the tents up in record time. The following day we had arrived at our third scheduled campsite and were looking forward to reaching our destination of Tossa de Mar on the east coast of Spain on the following day.

Back in the car the next day, we were getting restless. Dad enjoyed the drive, but he knew that it was hard on Mum and us, but also he knew that when we reached the destination and were on the white sands and splashing about in the warm blue water, it would all be worth it. Elizabeth didn't forget to remind Dad that he hadn't yet given us our prizes for spotting the Eiffel Tower. Although Dad was not in the habit of teasing us, he did wonder how long it would be before we gave up asking, at which point he would produce something nice for us.

The last leg of the journey to Tossa de Mar seemed to drag on, and as the roads became narrower and the weather increased to an almost unbearable heat, Dad began to question his decision to drive this far. It was an unusually hot summer, even by Spain's standards, and the tarmac on the roads had started to melt in the heat.

As we drove over the crest of the last hill before winding our way down to the seaside town, we could see the blue ocean ahead of us. It was a sight that I will never forget. There were two steep hillsides either side, which were covered in beautiful trees of all shades of green. The deep blue ocean contrasted with light blue sky, which had the odd white clouds floating within it.

We were as excited now as when we had set off just three days earlier. The campsite was just a short walk from the town and beach, but there were trees enough to provide the welcome shade that we would need to escape from the burning heat. Mum had brought plenty of suntan lotion, and had applied it just as soon as we were out of the car.

Dad and Jimmy configured the tents so that they were facing each other and close enough to spread the huge tarpaulin that Dad had brought along to provide extra shade.

It was now mid-afternoon and the sun was at its hottest. I collected pinecones and tried to catch grasshoppers with the other kids.

By the time the suitcases had been laid out, the temporary kitchens erected, the air beds pumped up and the paraffin lamps and cookers made ready, it was time to go and buy the provisions.

Although we pleaded to go and play on the beach and in the sea, the adults were more interested in keeping us fed and watered.

As we walked through the little town, it was clear that this was mainly a holiday destination for Spanish people; there were very few English families around. Dad and Victoria wanted us to experience some of the real local culture and had deliberately avoided the touristy towns.

We found a welcoming family-run café where we enjoyed seafood salads and ice-cold drinks, followed by ice cream and fresh fruit. The family who ran the café spanned four generations, and a return visit was promised.

Dad explained that we had to do the shopping before everything closed for the afternoon siesta. He was used to working outside and said that it would be very difficult to carry out any manual work in the afternoon heat.

We visited a few shops and Mum bought enough food to last a couple of days. We headed back to the campsite and, after unpacking what had been bought and getting us kids ready for bed, Mum suggested that Dad and Uncle Jimmy take a walk into town and take a look around. She knew that they would welcome the opportunity to have a cold beer, and she was looking forward to relaxing and chatting with Victoria while we settled down for the night.

Dad and Jimmy were not normally irresponsible, and would never knowingly stay in a bar too long, but on this occasion time did run away with them.

'Come on, Jimmy, let's just have a couple more; the girls will be enjoying being without us for a little while.'

Dad liked his beer, and it didn't take much to persuade Jimmy to stay.

It was eleven o'clock and very dark before they returned, a little bit on the drunken side but in a happy and giggly mood.

Although Mum didn't really mind, Aunty Victoria was not too pleased, and we all laughed when we heard Victoria giving Jimmy a telling-off.

When Dad got up in the morning, and came out of the tent stretching and enjoying the bright sunny morning, Jimmy was already out. As they looked at each other they found it difficult to stop themselves from breaking out into roars of laughter.

'Good morning, Jim,' said Dad, with just enough volume that Aunty Victoria could hear. 'How are you this morning?'

Jimmy looked at Dad, knowing very well that he was teasing him and trying to get him to laugh, which Jimmy was struggling not to do.

'Morning, Pat. I'm fine, thanks,' he said, giving Dad a knowing look.

'Morning, Vic,' Dad said through the thin canvas wall of the tent. He knew Victoria would still be angry with Jimmy, and although he wasn't trying to cause an argument, he also knew that Victoria wouldn't want to be seen as a nagging wife.

'Hi, Pat. Did you have a good night last night?' retorted Victoria, in a rather harsh but controlled voice.

Dad knew he should change the subject and quickly.

'Okay then, who's coming to the beach?'

With that, we clambered out of our sleeping bags. After eating a hurriedly prepared breakfast and securing the tents, we were off to the beach with our blow up beach balls, towels and large umbrellas. It was nine o'clock in the morning and still fairly cool.

The waves were almost unnoticeable, and the water was crystal clear as we enjoyed our first dip in the sea. There were no clouds in the sky and only a slight breeze coming off the sea.

The towels were laid out under the umbrellas and we all found it difficult walking from the shade of the umbrellas to the water because the sand was scorching.

Mum had put a little white hat on John, and was enjoying the cool water as she dipped up and down to her shoulders with John in her arms.

As planned, after a few fun-filled hours on the beach, we headed back to the campsite to hang out the wet clothing and towels, before having a snack and going into the wooded hills. In the evening, we went back to town to eat and drink at the family café we discovered on the previous day.

The holiday continued in this way, with trips up the hillside and into the mountains and to other towns and beaches. By the time to pack up and leave came, we all had dark tans and happy hearts.

We took a slightly different route on the way back, but it was uneventful and enjoyable because the weather had become slightly cooler.

We begged our parents to take us to Spain again, and they seemed to agree to it.

*

Back home, our friends and neighbours all commented on how nice we looked. I took great delight in showing people the top of my buttock cheeks, which were as white as snow in comparison with the rest of my body. This was the cause of much amusement for quite a few weeks before the tan started to wear off.

Dad returned to work on a building site as a bricklayer. He had brought back with him several sombreros, which he passed around his workmates. They looked an odd bunch as they sang along to the radio in their sombreros.

As soon as we got home, Dad and Uncle Jimmy sent their films off to be developed, and the next few weeks and months included family get-togethers where we would have great fun watching ourselves on the big, white screen that Jimmy had set up in his living room.

Mum had very few photographs of herself as a child, and she didn't look happy in the ones she had, so it was very important to her that our happiness was captured on film.

Nan and Granddad often asked to see the holiday photographs, but Mum always made excuses. I didn't realise it at the time, but she could not let Granddad see Elizabeth in her swimming costume, as it brought back vivid memories of herself at eight years old, which she tried so often to erase from her mind.

Her father had taken her swimming during the summer months, and all she could remember was how he insisted on removing her swimming costume and drying her himself. She was not going to expose Elizabeth or any of us to him, even in photographs.

7

FAMILY FUN

My brother David was born in September 1966 and again Mum made sure that we all got involved in this very special event.

Mum was now enjoying the best time of her life, and she loved spending time with us kids more than ever before. In the ten years since Mum first gave birth, her life had changed immeasurably, and she threw everything into motherhood. Never a day went by without her smiling and being thankful for having such a wonderful husband. Their devotion and open affection for each other was apparent, and we grew up understanding how to express our own emotions with natural ease.

Mum knew it was important for us kids to bond, and there was never any jealousy between us. We did squabble, as can be expected from kids generally, but overall we loved to play and laugh.

Mum taught us at an early age that sharing was important, and the house was hardly ever in turmoil as a result of bickering or fighting. We were never exposed to any adult arguments. No doubt there *were* disagreements, but we would never have known about them at this point in time.

*

Dad expanded his business and was working as a self-employed bricklayer building new houses for private clients. Elizabeth was now ten, I was nine, John was three and David was now two, we were all content and loved life.

Mum was happy on the large council estate that we had recently moved to, there was a good atmosphere amongst the neighbours.

61

Everyone pulled together and were happy to help each other out whenever the need arose. The families on the estate tended to stay for years. The houses were well built and had large gardens, schools were close by, and there were plenty of local shops and recreation areas. Mum never worried too much, as there were plenty of older kids on the estate who kept an eye on the younger ones. It was a very working-class area; many of the parents had forged strong friendships and often worked together.

The estate had several grassy play areas, and it was not unusual for Dad to arrange a tug of war, or skipping competitions with the local Mums and Dads and all the kids on the estate.

Sometimes, Dad and one of the other fathers would climb the big oak tree on the green and rig up a rope and tyre for us to swing on, but this often caused arguments about whose turn it was. Dad would threaten to remove it unless we could share, which usually had the desired effect.

Dad also had a pickup truck, and he would allow some of the local children to sit on the back while he slowly drove us around the block. He would mimic the rag and bone man's cry of 'Any old iron? Any old rags?' which we found hilarious and would all copy.

On the odd occasion that some kids from other estates would turn up and cause problems for us, Dad and another of the parents would be on hand to move them on. Everybody on the estate looked out for each other, and Mum and Dad never really had to worry too much about where we were. If we weren't on the green, we would be in one of the neighbours' houses.

*

Dad got on with everyone around him and was a very colourful character; he made people laugh and was one of the most popular men on the estate. Whenever he had had a good run of work, and funds allowed, he would surprise us by announcing, 'We're going camping.'

He knew how to keep people entertained. Even in his work he could always be heard singing to songs on the radio. He was great fun to be around, and no one had a cross word to say about him.

From a very young age I looked up to my dad and wished I was like him.

Although Dad had loads of friends, he was devoted to us. His main aim in life was to make us all happy. I think many of our friends' parents were jealous of how happy my parents were.

Dad was a good looking man and always willing to help any of Mum's friends out with anything and even I could see that our friends mum's would enjoy his company. He made them laugh and although he probably did flirt, he only had eyes for Mum and she knew it.

Similarly, there had been a few occasions where other men had looked at Mum and smiled, which made Dad very angry.

On one occasion when we were very young, we were at a wedding reception, and on his return from the toilet he found a man talking to Mum. As he didn't know the man, he assumed that he was chatting Mum up. He mistakenly thought that she was enjoying the attention. Mum was very attractive, with a good figure, she always wore smart clothes and, without meaning to, she did often attract the gaze of other men.

Without any warning Dad punched the man, dragged him down some stairs and pushed him out of the door before returning to Mum and telling her that we were all going.

Mum loved Dad more than anything, and his jealousy was the only issue that they ever argued about. This incident did have an effect on Mum, as she felt slightly nervous when other men were around, just in case Dad mistook a smile for something very different. On the few occasions when Mum went out with a friend he would insist on taking her and picking her up. He had nothing to worry about, but it was his deep love for Mum that made him feel this way, or so he thought.

Dad had a huge family and would often take us to see our uncles and aunts. Between Dad and his brothers and sisters, they had produced twenty-six children and when we all got together for weddings or christenings, it was a big affair.

Dad's mum who we affectionately knew as *nanny with glasses* was respected and loved by us all, and although she *lived* alone, she was rarely *left* alone. Dad collected her every Tuesday evening to spend the evening and have dinner with us.

We also looked forward to her visits, as she always brought little gifts of sweets or would put a few coins in our hand as she left.

These were good times for everyone, but sometimes when Mum was feeling a bit depressed she would cuddle us and be more tactful than usual. We didn't know why at this stage, but we could feel that she was hurting. When she was like this, she didn't want to visit Nan and Granddad, which was a shame because Elizabeth and I loved walking their dog and feeding their parrot through the bars of the cage.

Nan and Granddad were always kind to us, and they had formed a real family bond with us, despite not seeing us very often. We had never even questioned why our grandparents never visited our house, or why they had never spent Christmas or had Sunday dinner with us.

It didn't really matter to us anyway, because there were so many other family members and friends to visit.

8

A COLD SHIVER RAN DOWN HER SPINE

Dad was naturally very protective of us, especially Elizabeth. When she started senior school, she wanted to walk home with her friends and hang out with them after school, but Dad wanted to take her and pick her up himself.

Mum could understand Elizabeth's frustration.

'Pat,' she began, 'I think Elizabeth needs a little of her own space. She feels that she can't be trusted to go to and from school on her own. Why not let her make her own way from now on, and we will see how she gets on?'

Dad knew that he had to give Elizabeth breathing space and wanted to make Mum happy.

'Okay love, I think she has quite a few friends now; providing she's not walking home on her own, I'm happy with that,' said Dad reassuringly to Mum.

'I'll speak to her later,' said Mum, 'and I'll tell her to get the bus if she has no one to walk with.'

Mum and Dad had no real reason to worry, as there had not been any reported incidents of bullying, but they knew what could happen if Elizabeth got in with the wrong crowd.

A few days later, the phone rang around about the time that Elizabeth was due home. Mum answered in her usual happy voice, 'Hello 36030.'

'Hello Mum, it's me. I'm at Nan and Granddad's house. I thought I'd call in and see them on the way home. Granddad is going to drop me off later.'

Mum's shoulders dropped, and a cold shiver ran down her spine. Elizabeth was nearly twelve years old and very pretty.

'No, darling, come home now. I have cooked dinner, and Karen has been round for you.' Mum was desperately trying to think of anything to get Elizabeth to come home now at once.

'Oh, Mum, please – Nan said I could eat here.'

'No, darling, I want you home *now*,' Mum was almost shouting. 'I'm not prepared to argue with you. Just get home now, and put your Nan on the phone.'

Elizabeth huffed.

'Mum wants to speak to you, Nan,' she said in a disappointed tone.

'Hello Mum. I'm sorry, but Elizabeth needs to come home now. Her friend is here waiting for her, and I have dinner in the oven.'

Nan knew exactly what Mum's real concerns were, but it was the unwritten rule that the past was not to be discussed.

Nan and Granddad lived just around the corner from the senior school where Elizabeth had started, but Mum had not given it a thought that she would pop in to see them.

Elizabeth started to walk home despondently, sure that she wasn't trusted to do anything. She was determined to speak to Mum about why she was not allowed to make her own decisions.

As Dad drove home he saw Elizabeth walking home on her own, and pulled over to give her a lift.

'Hello sweetheart, jump in.'

Elizabeth got in the car. Dad noticed straight away that she was not herself.

'How come you're walking home on your own, love? I thought you were getting the bus if you were alone.' He didn't want to seem too harsh, or to press the issue on her.

'Oh, it's Mum,' she said. 'I called in to see Nan and Granddad on the way home, and called Mum to say that Granddad was going to drop me off later, and she hit the roof!'

It was all Dad could do to keep his eyes on the road and not tell her why she must not go round to our grandparents alone.

'It's not fair, Dad, I am nearly twelve now and at seniors. When can I make some of my own decisions?'

Mum was waiting at the door, as they pulled up at the house.

'Hello love,' Dad said to Mum with a concerned look on his face.

'Hi,' Mum said as she kissed him on the cheek.

As their eyes met they knew that they were going to have to talk about the situation, and possibly to tell Elizabeth the truth.

That evening, when we had gone to bed, my parents had the conversation that they always knew they would have to have.

Elizabeth told me what had happened and we crept out of her bedroom onto the landing and tried as hard as we could to hear what they were saying. As hard as we tried we could barely make out what they were saying. John and David were already asleep and oblivious to what had happened.

'So what are we going to do?' we heard Dad say in a muffled voice. 'How can we tell her she mustn't call in to see them?'

'I'm going to tell her tomorrow,' Mum replied. 'She's old enough to understand, and I would rather tell her than lie to her.'

Intrigued we crept back to bed before our espionage could be discovered.

Mum had had a knot in her stomach. It was possible that her father had changed, but she wasn't prepared to risk it. She also knew what Dad would do to Granddad if the need arose.

The following morning just as Elizabeth was leaving for school, Mum saw her to the door.

'Darling, when you finish school today can you come straight home?' she said. 'I want to talk to you about something. You're not in trouble, but it's important.'

Elizabeth was not too worried, as she had often had chats with Mum on grown-up matters. They had a very close relationship and often discussed things that girls needed to know.

'Okay Mum, see you later.'

As she left for school, Elizabeth gave Mum a kiss. We were all very tactile and Mum always kissed anyone coming or going from the house.

I was still attending junior school, which was just around the corner from our house and despite finding it difficult at school academically, I was fairly well behaved and had not yet caused Mum and Dad too much worry.

Elizabeth arrived home at the usual time, and had forgotten about the chat she was due to have with Mum.

'Hi Mum,' she called as she bounded up the stairs, 'I'm just going to get changed. I'm going round to Karen's for a while. I'll be back for dinner.'

'Hang on, love, I need to talk to you.'

'Oh Mum, can't we talk later, please?'

Mum had to have the chat sooner rather than later, the knot in her stomach had intensified. She knew she had to talk to Elizabeth in order to feel better herself.

'Once we have had a chat, you can go round Karen's. I'll put dinner off for a while.'

Elizabeth changed and found Mum in the dining room waiting for her.

'Sit down love.'

Elizabeth sat down. She could sense that this was not going to be one of the simple chats that she had had with Mum on previous occasions.

'What's up, Mum?'

Mum hardly knew where to start, although she had been thinking about it all day.

'It's about your Granddad, love. I don't want you going round there on your own.'

Elizabeth was confused. They had visited many times and it had never been an issue before.

'When I was your age your granddad was not very nice to me.' Mum was struggling to put into words what she wanted to say. 'Your granddad was very strict, and I would often get a beating if he thought I had done anything wrong.'

Elizabeth knew that Mum was a kind and gentle person and couldn't imagine her doing anything that warranted a beating.

Mum couldn't hold herself together, and broke down in floods of tears.

'Mum, what's wrong?' Elizabeth said. She was really concerned now. 'Tell me, please – I'm scared.'

Mum tried to compose herself. Though she was still sobbing she knew she could not pretend any longer.

'Your granddad beat me and touched me in my intimate places; but I couldn't do anything about it, otherwise I would get more beatings.'

Elizabeth sat there in disbelief. Granddad had always been such a nice man.

'But, Mum, he's your Dad – why would he do that?'

Mum had never told us that she had been adopted, but now it was time to tell Elizabeth the truth.

'Well, darling Nan and Granddad are not my real parents, I was adopted at birth and I don't know who my real parents are.' Mum struggled to tell Elizabeth what she needed to know but as she spoke, she became more composed.

After an hour of talking, Mum was satisfied that Elizabeth understood what had happened, and that she mustn't talk about it to anyone.

Dad had taken the rest of us out so that Mum could have peace and quiet. He knew how difficult it was going to be for her. He had seen a complete change in her the night before; she became withdrawn and had not slept.

Dad knew that he would have to keep an eye on Mum and support her in every way he could as she faced her past.

*

Over the following few weeks we all noticed that Mum changed from her usual bubbly and happy self to become introverted and quiet.

'Come on, love,' said Dad one evening, trying to bring her out of her reverie when he caught Mum sitting at the dinning table just staring at the wall, 'Elizabeth won't be going round there on her own and if you don't want us to see them anymore, I will go and tell them.' Dad was prepared to keep the truce going, but only as long as it pleased Mum. He secretly wanted to administer his own form of punishment on Granddad.

That one occasion when he had pinned Granddad against the wall in the park shelter to warn him that his life would be in danger if he ever upset Mum again had certainly had an effect, but Mum knew nothing of this — it was his secret.

9

HE BROKE DOWN
IN TEARS

The next couple of years saw Mum become increasingly withdrawn. Dad would often find her sitting at the dining-room table in the early hours of the morning, looking through photo albums with tears in her eyes.

'Come on love, come back to bed.' He would plead with her to get some sleep. He was beginning to think that it was he who was responsible for the change in her, as he had started to drink more than usual, as it helped him to cope with the change in her.

Dad would often ask himself what he had done, or not done, but he failed to make any sense of it.

He confided in Aunty Victoria.

'Pat, she's just feeling lonely now that the kids are at school.' She was trying to say the right things, but in truth she had no idea why Mum was feeling so low.

'Can you pop round and speak to her, Victoria?' Dad asked. 'Maybe she will talk to you.'

Victoria promised she would try and help. She knew that Mum had not been treated well as a child, but had no idea how bad things had been. Dad had kept his promise never to divulge the details of what Granddad had done to her, but his promise was beginning to weigh on him.

Victoria kept *her* promise and called round to see Mum.

Mum opened the door, and as soon as she saw Victoria she had an idea why she was there.

'Hello Rose, just thought I'd pop round for a cuppa.' Aunty Victoria wasn't in the habit of calling round, and had decided to get straight to the point.

When Mum had made a cup of tea, they exchanged a few words about how the kids were and some general chitchat, Victoria started her tactful but obvious line of questioning.

'Pat tells me you've not been feeling too good of late. Is there anything I can help you with, Rose? He's worried about you, and feels that he is to blame.'

Dad had given Victoria a free hand to say what she felt was the right thing; he trusted her and was desperate to know what was so wrong with Mum.

'It's not Pat. To be honest I don't know what it is. I just feel like crying all the time, and I'm having trouble sleeping.'

Victoria could understand the situation as she had had a short spell of depression herself, and she too had not been able to link it to any particular event. So although she was at a loss as to what to say, she knew she had to provide some sort of support.

'Why don't you let Rick and Elizabeth come and stay with me for a while, to give you a rest? I'm sure they will enjoy it, and I'm due some time off work.'

Victoria had two sons and a daughter of her own, and they lived in a large house, so there was plenty of room to put Elizabeth and me up for a week or two. It had been Dad who had suggested the idea to give Mum time to relax and he knew we would have great fun with our cousins. We were happy to go to Aunty Victoria's and although we knew things were not brilliant at home, the thought of being with our cousins for two weeks, and the fun we could get up to, was exciting.

The atmosphere between Mum and Dad worsened over the next few months. Mum could not shake off her depression, and Dad started to drink regularly; he would more often than not arrive home late for the evening meal to find Mum subdued and quietly tearful. Although rows and voices raised in anger were never part of family life, we had begun to notice the tension.

I had seen the change in Mum's demeanour, and often tried to cheer her up with my usual antics. Sometimes I would hide things, sometimes I would tickle her, which previously she would have found amusing. Now she found it difficult to find anything funny, although she tried to join in the fun. I was very close to Mum, and was worried about her, but I was unsure what I could do to help her, which upset me.

Elizabeth tried to talk to Mum as well, but she too couldn't make a difference.

Although Elizabeth knew what Mum had been through as a child and suspected what was behind Mum's depression, it was probably more difficult for her as she had to keep that secret.

We did stay with our aunt from time to time, but it only made Mum unhappier and more anxious, as she felt that she had failed us. She was now spiralling into a deeper level of depression, and Dad knew that he had to do something drastic. Things were affecting him and he often took them out on us when he was drunk. He never hit us, but it seemed that we could never do anything to please him.

Mum had been to a doctor who had prescribed antidepressants, but they were having little or no effect. She was getting very little sleep at night, at one point, she had not slept at all for two weeks solid. Dad decided to make an emergency appointment with the doctor.

'I want something else done,' Dad pleaded with the doctor.

The doctor told him he would prescribe further antidepressants.

'They're not working!' shouted Dad. 'I'm watching my wife change into a different person.' Dad was a strong-minded man and never normally showed his emotions on this level, but he could not hold it in any longer. He broke down in tears and dropped to his knees in front of the doctor.

The doctor knew he would need to take a different line of approach and consider treating Dad for mild depression too, for now though he had to concentrate his efforts on Mum.

'I am going to refer Rose to a psychiatrist.'

'I am sorry for my outburst, doctor, but I just don't know what to do any more.'

'I will speak to the appropriate people to have Rose assessed, but I think it would also be good if you made an appointment to see me about how you are feeling.'

Dad left the doctor's surgery after making an appointment for himself and happy in the knowledge that Mum's treatment would change, though he was honest enough to admit that he had no idea whether it would work. He felt so ashamed both of his breakdown and the fact that he had gone behind Mum's back, that over the next few days he found it difficult to talk to anyone.

Dad did go to see the doctor and was put on a mild dose of antidepressants, which helped but Dad couldn't help feeling guilty for having succumbed to depression. He thought of himself as a strong man and didn't like the weakness that he could see developing.

Dad got us together when Mum was in bed one evening.

'Mum is going away for a while to a relaxing hospital where she will get the correct treatment to help her get back to normal.'

Elizabeth had already been told as she was the eldest and Dad knew that he would need her help more than ever.

I felt a knot immediately form in my stomach. 'What do you mean Dad?' I asked.

'How long for? Where? Why?'

My mind was racing, I knew that Mum was not well, but to hear that she needed to go to hospital was a total shock. Tears filled my eyes and I ran up to my room.

John and David were of the age where they didn't understand the full gravity of the situation although they were frightened by the news.

Dad explained things to them as best he could and they accepted his word readily.

Elizabeth came to my room and tried to console me.

'Don't worry Rick, it's all for the best you know. You've seen how Mum has gotten worse lately.'

'But why Elizabeth?' I asked, really not understanding what had gone so very wrong.

'You will understand one day Rick, believe me.'

I didn't pick up on what Elizabeth had said and I am sure that she came very close to telling me about what Mum had endured as a child, but her promise was to hold until Mum agreed to let us boys know the truth.

A week later Dad took Mum to see the psychiatrist she had been referred to. He was glad to know that she was to be admitted to a psychiatric unit straight away where she would be assessed and monitored and given medication that would ensure she slept.

Mum was not in a fit state to argue, and trusted Dad implicitly when he told her it was for the best.

Mum's initial admission to the psychiatric unit was to be for ten days and then a decision would be made for the length and type of treatment plan that she would need, based on the psychiatrist's assessment.

Most people in the surrounding towns saw the psychiatric unit as a place where people who were too unstable to live in the community were housed in secure units. Dad was shocked when he took Mum there for the first time, as all of the external doors were locked and could be opened only by the staff.

'It's just for security,' he was told. 'We sometimes get patients who are on heavy drugs who may be delirious and want to leave, so we prefer to keep the doors locked. Better safe than sorry, don't you think?'

This explanation put Dad at ease, and although Mum looked hesitant, he told her that she was in the best place she could be. He spent a couple of hours with her before she was shown to a bed in a ward that had several other women in it.

'I must go now,' he told her, 'but I'll be back tomorrow, about four o'clock.'

Mum held onto his arm so tightly that Dad was shocked at her strength. He knew he had to be mentally strong, and reassured her that she would soon be better.

They had never spent an evening apart in the fourteen years that they had been married, and Dad had to stop several times on the fifteen-mile drive home, as he could hardly see through the tears that streamed down his face. If it was hard on Mum he knew it was going to be hard on him too, and that it was down to him to help her get better.

Although it broke his heart, he had to think of what was best for the whole family, and he knew we needed a healthy mother.

That evening Mum was given an injection and couldn't quite understand why there were so many doctors and nurses standing around her bed, discussing her treatment.

As she lay in her bed she could feel herself drifting, and the voices became just echoes in her head. Although she was not quite awake, she knew they were bringing in equipment, and could hear the swish of the curtain being pulled around her bed. She felt as though she was in a dream, and could do nothing about the pushing and pulling from the doctors and nurses. She knew that someone had rubbed fluid on her temples, and that there was a rubber block in her mouth, and then the rest became a blank.

Dad had been told that her treatment would start that evening and that she would definitely sleep. This pleased him, and when he was told that she would be having ECT, he trusted that this was best for her; but he didn't actually ask what those letters stood for and assumed it was just some medication.

The following morning when Mum woke up, she was crying and very subdued.

'Nurse, nurse, please help me,' she said. 'I ache all over and my head hurts.' She tried to raise her voice, but she felt exhausted.

She lay on her bed for what she thought was a few minutes, when Dad appeared at her bedside.

'Hello love, how are you feeling?' Dad could see that she was not herself, but the nurse had told him that she had slept through the night and eaten her breakfast and lunch, and that her treatment was beginning to work, although for the moment she would show signs of delirium until the doctors had her treatment fully under control.

Dad tried again.

'How have you been today, love?'

'I've only just woken up,' Mum replied. 'I'm glad you could come this morning.'

Dad was confused. It was four o'clock in the afternoon, why did she think it was morning he thought to himself. Then he remembered what the nurse had said and dismissed it as his wife being confused.

He managed to get Mum up, and was allowed to take her outside in the early evening sun. It was warm outside, and all he wanted to do was be with her alone and cuddle her until she got better.

They sat on a bench by a very pretty garden bed with an array of flowers and talked generally about things, though Mum seemed not to take in much of what Dad was saying.

'Don't worry, love,' he said. 'Everything will be all right, I promise.' He felt helpless, and wasn't even sure whether what he was saying was true.

It was seven o'clock when he walked her back through the pretty grounds to the small building within the huge complex of secure buildings. It was evident to him that whatever drugs they had given her, they had made her more subdued but seemingly less anxious. He kissed her goodbye and left saying that he would be back at the same time tomorrow.

Mum was given another injection that evening and again she knew that doctors and nurses were active around her bed, but the next thing she knew was that she was being woken up for breakfast, which was set in a side room within the building.

Again she had the pounding headache and her whole body ached.

'Don't worry, Rose,' the nurse told her, 'it's just part of your treatment. It will soon subside.'

After five days of the same treatment it had left Mum feeling no better, Dad decided to enquire as to what this ECT medicine was.

'Oh, no, Mr Joyce, it's not medicine, it's electroconvulsive therapy. We call it "ECT" for short.'

Dad was confused.

'And what does it involve?' he asked.

After a detailed explanation of the ECT treatment and some of the side effects, Dad was not happy, but he knew he had to rely on the experts.

The first ten-day treatment plan was extended to fourteen days, and by the end of it Mum was showing signs of improvement and wanted to come home to see us.

Dad had decided not to take us up to see her while she was having ECT, as she had been looking and sounding worse during her stay than she had been when she was admitted. He did take Elizabeth at Mum's request, but it was kept a secret from us boys.

Mum was always smart and took pride in her appearance before she became ill, but since then had gradually lost the drive. During her stay in the psychiatric unit it left her completely and she had to be persuaded to take baths and wash her hair. But she knew that we were coming with Dad to pick her up, and had asked Dad to bring her makeup and some of her best clothes for the ride home.

Rather than take us into the building when he collected her, Dad had asked us to wait in the car park. The other women in the small building who were there for depression were at various stages of their treatment plans and some of them would often be heard crying during the day. Dad knew that we would not want our Mum to be in that sort of environment, and had never told us how bad she had felt at the start of her treatment.

PART TWO:

MUM COMES HOME

10

TENSION

As soon as Mum came out and saw us, her demeanour changed completely as we rushed to meet her. We all stood in the car park cuddling, and each of us had tears of absolute joy running down our cheeks. With me and David on one side and Elizabeth and John on the other we walked slowly to the car, and I could immediately see that Mum was feeling better than she had for a long time. Dad had told us not to fire all sorts of questions at Mum, and he also told us that it was likely that she would have to return to the special hospital at some point.

As soon as we were in the car, we were eager to give Mum the little presents that we had wrapped up for her. Mum enjoyed the ride home, and asked Dad if we could go home via the seaside and along the clifftop where we could see Kent on the other side of the River Thames. Dad was only too happy to do whatever she wanted.

It was six o'clock when we got home, and Dad had bought us all fish and chips. Elizabeth and I had thoroughly cleaned the house earlier in the day, and we had put up some "Welcome Home" banners that we had made. Dad had bought some flowers, and had them all ready in the vase in the living room. He would often buy flowers for Mum and knew she would enjoy seeing them.

Mum was eager to find out how we had been, and after dinner we all went into the living room and talked about anything that Mum wanted to, which was mainly about how we were doing at school and what we had been doing generally.

John and David went to bed at their usual time of eight thirty, and me and Elizabeth, Dad and Mum had a game of cards, which was something that we would often do before Mum became ill.

After me and Elizabeth had gone to bed, Mum snuggled up on the sofa with Dad and they both chatted about her illness and how it had affected us kids. Dad assured her that we were fine, and that although we missed her, we were enjoying school and being really good at home.

In reality Dad had struggled to cope with working on a building site during the day, visiting Mum in the evening and trying to keep on top of things at home, and it was starting to weigh heavily on him. He had become short-tempered with us, though he hadn't really noticed it, and we found it hard to adjust to having to do things that we were not used to doing. But we knew better than to argue with Dad, and though he never smacked us, his voice was enough to scare us.

Elizabeth and myself had been used to going out after school, but since Mum went into the psychiatric unit, we had to look after John and David until Dad got home from work. John and David were often taken to school and collected by a neighbour, who would look after them until either Elizabeth or I got home. Elizabeth in particular had to run baths, cook dinner, wash the clothes and hang them out to dry, iron shirts and look after the boys while Dad went up the hospital. My jobs were washing up, keeping the boys entertained and helping Elizabeth if I could.

Although we knew that we had to help out, it became very hard, and this caused problems between us. The boys would not argue much with Mum and Dad around, but when it came to doing as Elizabeth or I told them, it was a different thing.

It became clear to Dad that ill feelings were rising, as he would be told that the boys had been misbehaving while he was out, and when he saw the boys in the morning they would complain about Elizabeth and me.

All this added to Dad's other problems and tension was at a high before Mum came home. Dad knew that things would get better with Mum at home, but he was conscious that she needed rest. He took a couple of days off of work to spend time with Mum, and allowed us kids to go out when we got in from school while he prepared dinner. This improved the mood in the house, and Mum had no idea how tense things had been before her return.

It was now the weekend and Dad left it to Mum to decide what she wanted to do, which was not a lot. She was still suffering from the ECT, and was confused as to why she was struggling to remember things. She assumed it was the different medication that she was taking, which was helping her to sleep.

Dad had arranged for him and Mum to spend some time with John and David on their own, and took them to the zoo while me and Elizabeth did our own thing, which we were glad of. The weekend passed with us all getting back to our near-normal life, although I could tell that Mum was feeling worse as the days went on. She did not want to worry Dad, and convinced him that she was just tired. In truth she was feeling anxious and had heard voices in her head while she was awake.

Dad knew he had to keep working, and although things would become easier for us kids now that Mum was home, we each had jobs to do on our return from school before we were allowed out to play.

After two weeks it was clear to Dad that Mum was struggling to cope with life at home. She was sleeping less and less as the days went on, despite taking sleeping tablets, and she was starting to become weepy for no reason.

Although he did not want Mum to have to undergo more ECT treatment, he had been told it was likely that her treatment was going to take many weeks or even months before she would start to get back to normal.

A further two weeks passed, and Mum was in a similar state to that as when she first went to the psychiatric unit. Dad had no choice but to contact the psychiatrist to arrange for Mum to return for more treatment.

'I don't want to go back there, Pat,' said Mum, weeping in his arms.

'But, love, you will only get better if you have the treatment,' he told her half-heartedly.

Dad was not totally convinced of the effectiveness of the treatment, but he wanted to believe in it. It was clear that Mum was deteriorating by the day, and she had seemed better when she came home the first time.

So Mum returned to the psychiatric unit, and this time it was for three weeks, but she insisted that she be allowed home at the weekends.

Dad was really short tempered and when I asked why she had to go back, he tore my head off.

'Why has she got to go back? Don't fucking ask me,' he shouted at me with the look of someone I barely recognised.

I was as upset as him, but I couldn't work out why he was being so hard on us kids at times.

Mum's treatment was harsh and her memory was being affected, which only compounded her anxiety. When she came home for the weekends, she found it hard to carry out even menial tasks at home, and although her sleeping tablets were working, they made her tired all the time. She enjoyed the weekends as much as she could, and we gradually fell into what we took to be a normal life. We got used to Mum's change of demeanour, and would unwittingly add to her woes by taking our sibling arguments to her. Mum didn't want to tell Dad about our squabbling, as she hated the tension when he told us off. The cycle continued like this for weeks and months, with Mum spending two or three weeks at a time in the psychiatric unit and two or three weeks at home.

Home life changed for us all over this period. Dad was struggling to keep on top of things. He had taken to drinking regularly to help him shut out the truth that he was unable to make Mum better. Even though he had accepted the reality that this was how life would be from now on, his drinking had started to exacerbate matters.

We knew that if he had had a drink, we had to be on our guard and either behave or keep out of his way, which had an adverse effect that we could not see. Dad felt that we were avoiding him and didn't appreciate the good things that he had done in the past, but he was a different man completely when he was drunk or even slightly intoxicated.

In the days when Mum was well, having a drink made him feel good and he was great fun to be with, but with the added pressure of her being ill and not at home, together with his anti-depression medication, had quite a different effect. He became more aggressive towards Elizabeth and me for the slightest wrong-doing, and the atmosphere grew to fever pitch. He would often look for reasons to reprimand Elizabeth and me in particular, or so it seemed, but in reality we had not been helping out as much as we had when Mum first fell ill.

Quite often Elizabeth was sharply reprimanded for very minor incidents like not being home when she was expected, or not having shirts ironed for the boys for school the next day.

Many tears were shed during the next year or so and we seemed to be torn apart. I would often try to support Elizabeth if she was being told off, but Dad would turn on me and threaten to hit me, particularly if he had been drinking.

'Keep your nose out, Rick,' he would say, 'I run this house, and what I say goes.'

I started to feel that I hated Dad at times, and the change in him was hard to accept. I also wondered if Mum's illness was his fault—maybe he treated Mum as badly as he treated me. None of it seemed to make sense and although I would discuss things with Elizabeth, there was never a clear answer.

It was only during Mum's visits home that things improved, but she could not stay home in a comfortable state for more than three or four weeks at a time without having to go back.

She had to accept her routine and the treatment that she hated, and although the periods spent at home were gradually getting longer, she was starting to rely on the treatment and saw it as part of her life.

We too were getting used to the routine; and while only a couple of years before we had been a happy family unit, we were now a family struggling to cope with ordinary life. Dad would have spells of being totally in control and then spells of despair and silent depression. He would disappear for hours on end after visiting Mum, and we would often find him asleep on the settee in the morning, which caused us to worry. We didn't know what to do or say, and it was only when I mentioned to my Aunty Victoria that Dad was acting strangely that she decided to try and help.

Victoria thought that things had been going well, but that was only based on what Dad had told her.

'Come on, Pat, let's go and talk about things,' she said one day, on a visit to the house.

Dad was a proud man. He hated the thought of defeat, but with Victoria's intervention and persistence we started to get a routine together in which communication between us got better and we spent more time with other family members when Mum was in the psychiatric unit.

As time went on and the new routine started to work, things did get better, which was in part to do with Aunty Victoria's constant family support for us all.

She would often take us to visit Mum at the psychiatric unit during the week, not only for Mum's sake but also to give Dad some free time, even if it was only for an hour or so, and this soon started to be reflected in Mum's improved mood.

Dad had decided long before that he didn't think we would want to see Mum in the psychiatric unit, as she would often look dishevelled and tired.

'If only I had thought differently, would she still be there?' he reflected when Victoria told him how Mum came out of her reverie when she saw us.

A new approach was planned to help Mum's recovery: Dad decided to take us with him when he visited her. We looked forward to visiting Mum, and enjoyed seeing her as much as she did us.

Dad would often drive us to a local pub where we would sit in the garden and the other people around took us for a happy and normal family enjoying the evening.

But as the weeks and months continued, with Mum coming home and going back to the psychiatric unit for weeks on end, the excitement soon wore off. It seemed almost a chore to us, as Mum was never in a fit state to hold long conversations with us, either at the psychiatric unit or in the pub garden.

Dad soon realised that taking us was now having an adverse affect on Mum, as she would often cry when we had to leave. Although Mum was deemed fit enough to go home for weekends and for longer periods, she was on heavy medication to help her sleep at night, and had a nurse assigned to visit her at home regularly to monitor her condition.

Dad was told that the condition Mum had been diagnosed with was paranoid schizophrenia, which had probably been brought about by what she had endured as a child, having had to adopt a dual personality to shut out the torment and abuse.

The psychiatrists had had to tease this out of Mum over the months and years of her treatment in the psychiatric unit. It was only as a result of the methods that the dedicated doctors and nurses used to uncover the truth about her past and document them that eventually helped her to come to terms with it.

Dad already knew it, of course, but knowing that it had been recorded on paper made him want to take vengeance on her 'parents', as Mum referred to them, but he knew that this would only make matters worse. His main concern now was to ensure that Mum was not put under any undue pressure and when she was next at home and somewhat better, we all started to get back to an even keel. We could not have known that secretly Mum was still struggling with her demons as she kept it well hidden.

Mum was planning to end her life for our sakes; her demons had been telling her to take not only her own life but the life of her children too. She knew that she could not harm us, but so strong were the demons' words that she decided on a plan of action. She put her plan into action on a sunny summer's day after she had packed us off to school, and although she knew that she would not see us again there were no obvious signs to any of us. The voices in her head were so powerful that they overruled any logical sense, and even blocked any emotions that she would normally have shown.

It was a thirty-minute walk to the seaside and the cliffs that she knew so well, and where she had often taken us when we were younger. The cliffs were not sheer, as the name suggests, but a series of winding paths and rockeries, with beautiful flowers and a range of exotic trees, with benches where people would sit and read or just watch the ships and sailing boats pass by.

Mum knew very well that her medication was extremely strong, and that a large dose of the sleeping tablets and other medication that she had to take every day would be enough to put her out of her misery and allow us all to be rid of her and start to enjoy life again. It would be a blessing to her too, as she really did feel that she was making our lives miserable – these were the types of messages that the voices in her head were telling her.

'Why should they have to put up with me crying and not being there for them?' she would often think to herself. She knew Dad loved her, but memories of recent tensions and his bouts of drinking clouded any reasonable thought that she might have been able to summon up. She thought that ending it now was the only option left. It would mean that she would not have to endure another ECT treatment that she hated so much, and the voices in her head would be silenced at last.

She sat down on a little blanket under the shade of a tree away from other people, opened her bag, and took out the little containers holding the various tablets that would end her misery. She had things well planned, and opened the bottle of water that she had brought along and swallowed the tablets one by one until they were all gone. She knew that it would not take long for her to gently fall asleep, and she imagined that other people would just think she was enjoying the summer's day relaxing on the cliffs.

As she drifted off to sleep, she did not get emotional, as she was already in a state of numbness, which was how she often described herself. After about an hour her breathing had become very shallow and a passer-by was concerned that if she lay there much longer she would be quite burned by the heat of the sun that was now shining on her face.

He walked towards Mum. As he approached her he could see the empty containers around her. They were obviously for medication, and he knew straight away that there was something more sinister going on. He called to a woman who was walking her dog not far away, and asked her to watch over her while he raised the alarm.

The hospital was only a couple of miles away, and the ambulance arrived within five minutes. The paramedics soon realised that Mum was very close to death, and raced her to the intensive care unit within minutes of assessing her condition.

The hospital staff took over from the ambulance crew on their arrival, while a police officer that had been sent for searched through the bag that had been found by Mum's side.

Mum had always carried a little address book in her bag, and within half an hour they had managed to contact Aunty Victoria. She managed to track Dad down on a building site in the town. While he rushed to Mum's side, Victoria picked me and Elizabeth up from school.

Elizabeth attended a different school to me, but it was just on the other side of the street. Aunty Victoria had decided to pick Elizabeth up first and had already explained what had happened to Mum before they came to get me.

As soon as I saw them both standing there, I knew something terrible had happened but I had no idea how serious things were. I can recall an instant feeling of fear in the pit of my stomach and I was unable to speak.

'Sit down love,' Aunty Victoria said. We were in the headmaster's office and I sat down fearing the worst. 'Your Mum has been taken to hospital and she needs you and your sister there now.'

Aunty Victoria knew that she couldn't go into detail there and then and told me that she would explain more on the way to the hospital. After the initial shock and comforting words we were off to the hospital. Things were explained to us in more detail on the short journey to the hospital, but we were not ready for what awaited us.

It was difficult for our Aunt as she had been informed that it was unlikely that Mum would survive – she just hoped that we could cope with what we were about to face.

Victoria had arranged for the younger boys to be picked up from the junior school and dropped off at her own house, where a friend had been waiting to look after them. It was agreed that they were too young to go to the intensive care unit and see Mum so close to death. They had just been told that Mum was very ill and had been taken to hospital.

We walked into the unit, where Dad was caressing Mum's hands and willing her to wake up and smile at him.

Tears streaked our faces as we stood looking down at our Mum lying pale and motionless in the hospital bed, I remembered how she had hugged me and waved me off to school only a few hours before. I couldn't comprehend what could have happened in those few hours. We didn't need the softly spoken nurse to tell us that our Mum was not expected to live, the hushed tones of those around us, and the complicated web of tubes and hospital machinery that surrounded Mum, had already made that clear.

My mind refused to absorb the shock, and my bewilderment only increased when I was told that she had been found unconscious on the cliffs with empty pill bottles beside her.

Elizabeth was in a state of shock and as she held Mum's limp hand she quietly prayed for her to get better and to open her eyes.

Victoria eventually took us back to her own house, leaving Dad to spend time alone with Mum in her last few hours of life.

The next few days passed with a subdued atmosphere that affected the whole family. Dad's brothers and sisters offered their total support and helped to look after us.

The doctors were surprised to find that they did not have to switch off Mum's life support machine as they had been expecting. A kindly nurse explained to us that they had attached a little tube through her throat to make sure she could get air into her lungs. The array of machines and equipment that had kept her alive were making noises that gave everyone hope.

Days passed by and Dad spent every waking hour by Mum's side. He did call in to see his brothers and sisters, where we had been staying, just to tell us that Mum was hanging on and that the doctors were doing everything they could.

Dad was not really a religious man, but he found himself praying as he had never done before; so when the doctors told him that Mum was going to be taken to a side ward and out of intensive care, he broke down and sobbed uncontrollably with a happiness that he had never experienced.

'Your wife is going to be okay,' one of the doctors told him. 'There doesn't appear to be any brain damage, but until we can allow her to gain full consciousness we shan't know fully the extent of any damage.' Mum was being kept semi-conscious until her body recovered sufficiently for her to come off the heavy drugs gradually and gain consciousness naturally.

Dad told us all the good news, but he warned us that the recovery period was going to be long and difficult. As before, our aunts and uncles assured him that he could rely on them for any support.

As Mum began her recovery in hospital, we eventually resumed our home life, and Dad began his role in taking care of us on his own. He was a popular man, and offers of support came from all directions, including anything from offers of food and money to weekends away for us kids, and many other small but significant offers.

Things were going to have to change. He knew that yet again Elizabeth and I would need to help him to run the house and look after John and David.

Having to carry on working to provide for us and ensure that we were fed and had clean clothes soon began to take its toll again. He felt guilty about having to ask Elizabeth and I to do so much, and began to realise even more than ever how much he had relied on Mum for her mothering skills.

Dad visited Mum every night in the hospital during the six weeks she was there, and was happy that we could visit her with him whenever we wanted to. He had arranged "Welcome Home" banners in the house on the day that he brought Mum home, and had also invited some close family members who he knew Mum would want to see.

Mum could not talk, as the tracheotomy operation had still to heal, so it was hard for her not to be able to tell us how much she loved us and that she was so sorry for what she had put us all through.

Mum had to write everything she wanted to say down on paper, which was difficult for her, but she so desperately wanted to say it.

We were just happy to have her back home again, as our life had been turned upside down emotionally as well as in all other ways. We had been well looked after by aunts and uncles, neighbours and friends while Mum was in hospital and Dad had made sure we saw her as often as possible. He knew what we meant to her, despite her irrational decision to try to take her own life. He never knew that her demons had been telling her to kill her own children, for Mum took those secrets to her grave. They would only be uncovered in doctors' and psychiatrists' notes some years later.

All Dad knew was that he had to work harder than ever to keep Mum safe and free from stress and any other problems.

As we grew older, communication between us was better than it had been for a long time. Although Mum still felt depressed she no longer felt suicidal; her medication had been changed and strict controls were put in place for her to take them. A nurse had been assigned to visit her at home every day to administer the drugs until constant monitoring confirmed that they were having a positive effect.

After about eight months at home, Mum suggested that she would benefit from spending time in the psychiatric unit – but without having to have the ECT treatment. Her doctor agreed to this, on the basis that she was starting to make rational decisions. He could see that she was still fragile, but she did not appear to be in danger of harming herself again.

What had led her to that decision was that she felt that being at home was making her ill, as she was starting to hear voices when she was alone. There had also been some arguments at home between me and Dad and more so Elizabeth and Dad. For some reason we could not please him, despite trying very hard to keep out of his way and help around the house. Dad was getting worse. His drinking had continued, and it was when he came home from the pub that he seemed to pick on us for no reason.

One day while Mum was in the psychiatric unit, Dad had been out drinking heavily after work, and when he came home to find John and David in bed and Elizabeth in the house with a friend. He told the friend to leave and shouted, ranted and raved at her.

'Who told you that you could bring friends in this house?' he yelled. He was angry and his voice was frightening.

'But, Dad, we were only looking after John and—'

Elizabeth didn't get time to finish what she was saying, for Dad grabbed her by the arm and marched her to the bottom of the stairs.

'Now get up there,' he told her, 'and don't let me see your face again this evening.'

Elizabeth couldn't believe it. Dad had never been physical, and though he had not hurt her, he was strong, and she could feel the power in his hands.

After her friend hurriedly left the house, I came in by the front door and could feel the tension instantly.

'What's happened?' I asked innocently.

'What's happened? I'll tell you what happened, son,' yelled Dad as he approached me with a violent look on his face. 'This is my house, and if you bring anyone in this house without asking me, you'll get the same treatment.'

As Dad got within inches of my face, shouting loudly, I instinctively punched him in the face, something I had never contemplated before.

Dad fell back and in his drunken state he fell in a heap on the floor.

'Why are you picking on me?' I shouted as I stood over him lying on the floor. 'I'm not scared of you, Dad.' I was shaking with anger and fear, despite saying I wasn't scared.

'Stop it! Stop it, please!' shouted Elizabeth from the top of the stairs.

I was expecting Dad to get up and start to hit me, but he didn't; he just lay there looking up at me while Elizabeth looked down from the landing.

The shock of what had just happened had a sobering effect on Dad. He knew at that point that he had crossed a line that he never thought he would.

'Just go to bed,' he said softly as he slowly raised himself from the floor.

Elizabeth and me went to our rooms totally bewildered. Despite the emotional roller coaster of recent years, we were at a loss as to what to do.

The night was long, we hardly slept. I heard Dad get up in the morning, and could hear the spoon stirring the teacup as I went gingerly downstairs, not knowing what to expect.

As I walked into the kitchen and looked into the dining room, knowing that Dad would be sitting at the head of the table, I was nervous. As soon as I saw Dad I knew that my punch had landed with much more force than I had imagined the evening before.

'You landed a good punch on me last night, son,' said Dad calmly. 'It's nice to know you can look after yourself if you need to.'

I didn't know what to say or do. Dad's top lip was swollen badly and his face looked quite disfigured. I knew that I would not stand a chance against him in a real fight, and after the initial shock of seeing him I felt quite guilty and ashamed.

Dad apologised for the night before, and when Elizabeth came down from upstairs he asked us both to sit down.

'I've been going to a doctor for depression for a few months now, and I know I have not been a good father to you both just lately.'

This came as a great shock to us, as he had always said he didn't like taking medication for anything.

'I can promise you now that I will change,' he told us, 'but I am really struggling without Mum being here.' He asked us both to keep from her what had happened, adding that he would tell her when she was well enough, and that he was fully to blame.

11

A FRAGILE STATE OF MIND

Dad decided to take the next day off and take the boys to school before he went to see Mum.

The shame that he felt from the night before and his own fragile state of mind were too much for him, and he broke down in tears when they were alone together. Mum knew he could be very intimidating with his words and his demeanour, especially when he had had a drink, but for him to admit it and be reduced to tears was something quite new to her. It was in a way the kick-start that Mum needed to force herself to get better, as she was and always had been the person that held us all together, if only she had realisedit. Dad was in a completely different state of mind from anything she had ever seen in him; it was almost a role reversal, she having to console *him* for a change.

Dad opened up. Although there were no real issues with the younger boys, he openly admitted that Mum's relationship with me made him very jealous. He had witnessed how we would often have fun with silly things, like when I would tickle her, or pick her up and put her over my shoulder, which always made her laugh.

I would tease Mum and Elizabeth in many ways, and they would pin me down and pinch the skin on the inside of my legs, but we would all be laughing and enjoying the closeness that we had. Little did we know that Dad wished he could make Mum laugh like that, as he used to when she was well and when they were both much younger. The financial aspects of Dad's responsibilities were at the top of his priorities; he wanted to ensure that we all had whatever he could afford, which he did despite the difficult circumstances. We were all treated the same, and although we perhaps didn't realise it, he wanted the best for us, and worked hard to make it happen.

His jealousy was not something that he could control but it manifested itself in ways that he had not realized, and it only ever came out when he had been drinking.

'Why doesn't he tell *me* the things he tells *you*?' Dad asked. 'He always talks about you, and you always talk about him or Elizabeth, so what about me?'

Mum could see that he was very upset about the situation, and on my next visit she reminded me that it would be good if I could talk to Dad more about things in general, and perhaps confide in him more.

Mum knew there had been problems, but she had not known to what depth and for how long.

We all looked forward to birthdays, and Dad always managed to make them special and to provide the things that we really wanted. Even if it wasn't top of the range, we were never disappointed with what we got. On my sixteenth birthday Dad had saved up and surprised me with a moped. Some of my friends had mopeds, and I had been hoping that Dad would be able to buy one for me. Elizabeth got one for her sixteenth, but I really wasn't sure Dad would be able to afford one for me.

Dad and Mum had always encouraged us to earn our privileges rather than just expect them, and the mopeds were bought on the condition that we took part-time jobs so we could afford to run and maintain them.

When Elizabeth got her moped she got a part-time job in a large high street store, which eventually led to a full-time position with promotion to management when she left school a year later.

I got a cleaning job to pay my way, and when I left school I went to work with Dad on the building sites. That brought its own set of problems, but Dad was happy that I was earning good money and following in his footsteps.

Having transport made a great difference to both Elizabeth and myself. It meant for one thing that we could visit Mum in the psychiatric unit when we wanted to, and Mum loved to see us. On one particular visit I asked Mum for advice about what I should do when I left school, which I was always prone to do. I knew she would always provide me with the words that I needed to hear.

I wasn't a mature sixteen-year-old, and needed guidance that to me, only Mum could provide. Mum was conscious that I would never ask Dad for personal advice, and this was in part because Dad was a man's man and not so good at being tactile or emotional.

When we were young it was very different, and he would hold us and cuddle us, but as we got older this disappeared. It wasn't that he couldn't offer emotional advice, but rather that he wanted us to stand on our own two feet and tackle life head-on as he had had to do.

Having subtly told me that Dad wanted to be closer to me and for me to confide in him more, Mum explained that it would cement our relationship. I took this advice on board, and despite not fully understanding what it meant, it did register and would be put to the test at some stage, although I felt that my relationship with Dad was good for the most part, despite his drinking.

Elizabeth's relationship with Dad was constantly strained as she entered her eighteenth year and was starting to meet up with her friends and boys of the same age. She wanted to bring her friends home, and when Mum came home for weekends it was never a problem, but when Mum was back in the psychiatric unit, she was fearful of Dad's reaction, and would only invite them round when he was out.

On one occasion, when Elizabeth was certain that Dad would not be home until late, she had invited a boyfriend around for a couple of hours while she was looking after John and David. She waited until the boys had gone to bed before letting her boyfriend in, and while they were watching TV, Dad came home unexpectedly.

Elizabeth heard his car pull up, and, recalling what had happened a couple of years previously, she told her boyfriend to leave by the back door.

Dad had brought me home, as we had been out playing snooker. While Dad was locking the car, I went to the front door and looked through the letterbox.

'Dad, quick!' I said. 'There's someone going out of the back door!' I shouted instinctively.

Dad ran down the side of the house and chased Elizabeth's boyfriend across the neighbouring gardens, but was unable to catch him.

I had not wanted to get Elizabeth in trouble, and this was something I regretted doing for a long time afterwards. Our relationship had always been close, but my impulsive action was going to drive a wedge between us for many months to come. To this day I really don't know why I told Dad what I had seen. I knew Elizabeth was looking after the boys and was shocked to see someone going out of the back door.

Dad was livid that Elizabeth had invited a boy back to the house while he was out, and it reignited the bad relations that had diminished over the past year or so.

I knew instantly that I was responsible for a situation that was not fair to my sister and that there was no way she deserved the torrent of verbal abuse that she had to endure from Dad.

Elizabeth wouldn't speak to me for a long time after this. I knew that Mum would be upset by what I had done, which hurt me more than anything.

Elizabeth was very mature for her age, and knew that she had to keep certain things from Mum. Although I thought my relationship with Mum was special, I never realized that Elizabeth's relationship was as strong if not stronger. It was only later in life when I matured that this would become clear to me.

Despite their difficulties, Elizabeth tried very hard to please Dad and would take Mum's role in relationship to the boys.

*

As time passed Elizabeth met and fell in love with a young man who Dad and Mum took to with ease. He was articulate and very different from the local boys who Elizabeth had mixed with in the past. Not that there was anything wrong with the local boys, but as far as Dad and Mum were concerned us kids were their life; they just wanted us to be safe and have the type of relationship that they had had in their early days, which was based on trust and true love.

Elizabeth's new boyfriend, Francis, soon became a part of the family. He showed interest in John and David and would take them on outings with Elizabeth, and he soon became good friends with me.

Mum was overjoyed to see Elizabeth so happy, and Dad too felt confident that Elizabeth had made a good choice. It was clear to him that she was in love and that Francis's support was unconditional.

Francis knew what we had all endured. He too had been through difficult times, having lost his parents at a young age. Although he kept this to himself, it meant he was very understanding and helpful to us as a family.

Although Dad wanted us to be happy, he was jealous of the freedom Elizabeth and I now enjoyed, and found it difficult to show an interest when we told him what we had been up to.

I had a new girlfriend and had decided to take her home to meet Dad before introducing her to Mum. I thought this would be a way of breaking the ice and getting Dad and I talking more freely. I asked Dad whether I could bring her round, and I offered to look after the boys while he visited Mum.

'Dad, this is Anne,' I said when I walked in the door after meeting her off the bus.

'Hello Mr Joyce,' said Anne.

'Call me Pat,' Dad told her. 'We don't stand on ceremony here, you know.' Dad was very agreeable and although he had been against Elizabeth bringing boy's home, it had never been an issue for me to bring girls home.

The atmosphere was instantly one of humour, and I was glad of my decision to introduce Anne to Dad first. Dad went off to see Mum and when he told her that he had met Anne and how nice she was, Mum knew that I was trying to repair the relationship between me and Dad.

Dad returned home in a good mood, and decided not to go for a drink, as he would normally do after visiting Mum. Instead he spent about an hour chatting to Anne and me, and when Anne said it was time she went, as she had to get two buses, Dad offered to run her home.

'No, it's okay, Pat,' she said. 'I wouldn't want to put you out.'

'Don't worry about that,' Dad said.

'Honest, Anne,' I said, 'Dad really doesn't mind, he'd rather run you home than have you spend over an hour getting buses.'

'Okay,' she said. 'If you're sure.'

'Elizabeth will be home in about half an hour,' said Dad, 'so she can look after the boys while we run you home.'

Elizabeth came home at her planned time, and Dad and me took Anne home.

'Thanks for running Anne home, Dad,' I said on the way back. In a few short hours something had happened that made the tense atmosphere that was usually present in the house completely disappear.

When we got home both Dad and Elizabeth were complimentary about Anne. She was very pretty and polite, and had made a good impression on Dad, who would eventually be her father-in-law.

The next few months went by without any real problems in the house. My relationship with Dad had improved tenfold and we often went to the little fishing village and wandered around looking at the boats, but when I decided to confide in him about a personal issue it undid several months of calm.

Anne and I had been out for the evening, and had returned home to Anne's parents' house quite late. Anne's Dad was a postman and he and Anne's Mum were always in bed by nine thirty. Anne put a video on, and we cuddled up on the settee to watch the film. It wasn't too long before we were in a passionate clinch, with various items of clothing having been removed.

I heard the living-room door open slowly. As I turned around I saw Anne's Mum standing there.

'Get your clothes on and get out of here *now*,' she told me in no uncertain terms. 'And you get up to your room *now*, Anne.'

I had my clothes back on and was out of the door within the blink of an eye, and set off home on my moped wondering how I was going to deal with the situation.

Anne's Mum and Dad liked me a great deal. I was always a bit cheeky, but happy to help out with anything I could. Anne's Mum particularly liked my sense of humour, and as I had grown up in a very tactile environment in which I would kiss Mum or my aunts whenever I entered or left the house, so I did with Anne's Mum.

Anne did have a brother living at home who was the same age as me, but they were not close or tactile with each other, and even Anne didn't kiss her Mum or Dad affectionately, except at celebration times like birthdays and Christmas. It wasn't that she didn't want to kiss them; it just wasn't something that her family done, so she really enjoyed coming to our house as Mum would always give her a hug and a kiss on the cheek when she arrived or left.

When I got home after Anne's Mum catching us on the settee, I found Dad still up and reading a book, which was unusual, as he was not an avid reader.

'Hello Dad,' I said as I entered the living room.

There was a strange atmosphere, one that I had experienced before when Dad and I were not getting on so well. To sense it now was odd, as things had been calm for a while.

On the way home I had made my mind up to confide in Dad, but I had not expected to be able to until the following day.

'Dad, I've got a slight problem,' I started, 'I was round Anne's house earlier, and when we were watching a film we got a bit passionate and took some clothes off. Then Anne's Mum walked in and caught us, and I'm not sure how I should apologize.'

I felt that asking for some fatherly advice would please him and Mum, but what happened next confirmed my justification for always confiding in Mum.

'You did what?' Dad shouted, as he got up out of his chair. 'You mean to tell me that Anne's parents open their door to you, and you abuse that privilege?'

Dad was standing in front of me now, and I could smell the alcohol on his breath.

'Dad, I'm asking for your advice.'

I was dumbfounded, and as Dad yelled in my face; I just let it wash over me. I remembered the time when I had hit Dad and how bad I had felt, so I took the volley of angry words. In any case I knew Dad's strength, and did not want to escalate things.

I went to bed and vowed never to confide in Dad again and to put the confrontation out of my mind. I decided that I would move into a flat of my own as soon as I could.

I lay awake for hours and worked out how I would apologise to Anne's Mum the following day. I knew her Dad would not say anything, even if he had been told, as he was a quiet man who did not like any confrontation even if he was in the right.

The following day I went to Anne's parent's house knowing that only Anne's Mum would be there. I was really nervous as I waited for the door to open, and when it did open I was surprised to hear Anne's Mum say, 'Hello Rick, I thought you'd be here today,' in a soft but stern voice.

'I'm really sorry about last night,' I said as I followed her into the kitchen.

'What's done is done,' she told me, 'but I don't want you doing it again in my house.' After a pause she added, 'Now, then, if you have time can you pop up the shop and get me some milk, please.'

I was shocked. I had expected a real dressing-down, and wished that my dad was so forgiving.

12

FUN WITH MUM AGAIN

Since the visit where Dad had been reduced to tears, Mum had been home on several occasions for a week or two at a time, and had felt the tension in the house when Dad and I were there together.

She was starting to feel better and tried to arrange longer visits home leading up to eventually being fully discharged from the psychiatric unit. She knew that harmony in the home depended on her providing the emotional stability that we all needed. However, she still felt that she had to go back to the psychiatric unit for short periods. She had become reliant on the unit, and although her sleep patterns were getting better, she was still not allowed to have lethal doses of strong tablets at home. Those that she could have were not as strong as the ones that were administered to her at the psychiatric unit.

She no longer had any thoughts of harming herself, and the voices in her head had long gone, but she still had bouts of depression that she had trouble shaking off without medication. Several times the doctors reduced her dose and tried other drugs, but it was a slow process to get it right.

Eventually the psychiatrists decided that Mum was well enough to be discharged from the psychiatric unit, as they had finally settled on a regular course of treatment that reduced the risk of her becoming addicted to the drugs and taking another overdose. She was assigned a nurse who would give her an injection every two weeks at home, and after just a few months the bubbly, smiling Mum that everyone had known seven years before began to re-emerge.

We could see the change in her week by week. No more would she sit and brood or be found sitting at the table crying; she could engage in conversation on all manner of topics, which she had not been able to do for years.

Even Mum could feel a difference in her demeanour, and enjoyed going out with Dad or Elizabeth and buying new clothes. She had not bought any new clothes for years, and had lost her interest in shopping.

Dad was feeling great; he could see Mum coming back into bloom just like a new rose itself. He worshipped the ground she walked on, but he knew that he hadn't been the perfect husband during the years that she was ill. He felt guilty about the times when, at his lowest ebb, he had nearly walked away from us all. I only found out about his uncharacteristic thought some years later when we were working together and talking generally about the past. But Mum was getting back to her old self now and these thoughts soon left him. Although he had tried to keep it from her, Mum knew that he was not well.

We were enjoying having fun with Mum again. We had forgotten how much fun she was, and although we teased her, it was always in good humour, and Mum took it as such. Even when I would swap the boiled eggs for fresh eggs that Mum had prepared for the salad, and laughed when she broke the shell to peel them, she couldn't help but enjoy in the practical joke.

Mum's laughter was something we had all missed so much.

On some occasions when Mum had gone into the garden to hang out the washing or water the flowers, I would lock her out and laugh out of the window at her.

'Come on, open it up!' she would say with a grin on her face.

'I can't find the key, Mum. Where have you put it?' would be my reply.

Mum secretly enjoyed all of this teasing, as it was something that she would have loved to be able to do to her own parents. But she never got angry about it – to see her own children laugh was more important to her than her getting upset with us. She knew that we had missed having fun with her, and she was surprised that she had not recognized it while she was ill.

'If only I could have thought of this when I was ill,' she said to herself, 'maybe I could have got better sooner, or perhaps not fallen ill at all.' She decided not to reflect too deeply on it, and resolved to enjoy life again and make up for all she had missed out on.

PART THREE:

A WHOLE FAMILY REUNITED

13

A SPECIAL MOMENT

I passed my driving test, bought a car, and moved into a flat with Anne, but still spent evenings and weekends visiting Mum, Dad and the boys.

Anne and I loved our new flat, which overlooked the sea. I had recently bought a windsurfer, which was something very new to the water sports scene. I would often go down to the beach with Anne after work to windsurf and enjoy the beach.

Mum and Dad were happy that I was settling down with Anne, and helped us with many of the things we would need. Dad moved us in and picked up some furniture for us in his truck.

It didn't take long for us to start to bond as a family again, once Mum showed that she was beating her illness. Although this was partly down to the help of regular medication, that seemed a small price to pay in exchange for being back together and enjoying one another's happiness.

Ever since Mum was told at the age of thirteen that she had been adopted, she had wondered what her real mother and father looked like, and although she had never discussed it at length with Dad, it was playing on her mind more and more. Her depth of depression and anxiety had mostly gone, but she still had those nagging thoughts about her real roots and whether she had any brothers or sisters.

Dad had decided there was something he could do. He made arrangements to go to the General Register Office at Somerset House, London, which was where he was told he could obtain Mum's birth certificate. Mum had asked her mother in 1965 for her birth certificate when she needed to apply for a passport to go to Spain, but was told that it had been lost many years before.

Nan lied to her – she had thrown the birth certificate in the fire many years before, as she didn't want Mum to know that she was given a different name at birth. She was also fearful that Mum would use it to track her real mother and break contact with her.

Mum managed to obtain her passport by providing her National Health Certificate and Marriage Certificate, but had she applied for her birth certificate, she would have found out who her real mother was many years beforehand.

Dad hoped to track down Mum's real parents through marriage certificates and any other records that he could find, but at the time when he visited Somerset House, the records were being transferred to the new General Register Office at St Catherine's House, London.

He was disappointed that he couldn't find the documents that he wanted, but he left Somerset House with renewed optimism. He had given as much information about Mum as he could, such as the area where she was born, her date of birth and who had adopted her originally, to a woman who had assured Dad that she would see what she could find and would forward the information on to him. She had taken a real interest in what Dad had told her, as she had been adopted herself, so she knew only too well what Mum was going through.

It was not until some six weeks later that a letter arrived for Dad in the early morning post. He had put his trip to Somerset House behind him, so it was a total shock when he opened the letter and found that it was Mum's birth certificate.

He was excited at the prospect of uncovering more information, and although there was a blank space where her real father's name should have been, he now had her mother's name and address at the time of her birth.

Mum had known that he had tried to obtain her birth certificate, and had got her hopes up; so when he returned empty-handed she became very tearful and was resigned to the fact that she would never know her real parents.

Dad decided not to tell her about the letter straight away, as this was something to celebrate.

'Okay, I'm off to work now, love,' he told her as he kissed her on the cheek. 'Why don't we go out for a meal this evening, I have a little something for you.'

'Yes, I'd like that, Pat. Have a nice day, and don't work too hard.'

Dad knew this would make her happy, and, much as he wanted to tell her there and then, he wanted to make it a special moment for her.

When Dad arrived home from work he found Mum in a really good mood. She was looking forward to going out. She loved to get dressed up, but it was not often that she felt in the right mood for it. She would try, but on some occasions when they had gone out, she had to pretend to be happy.

She could tell by Dad's tone of voice that he had something really special for her. She had no idea what it was, and had spent all day wondering what it might be. 'Is it a holiday?' she asked herself,. 'Or are we getting a new car?'

Elizabeth had offered to look after the boys. When Mum was ready and Dad had bathed and put on his best suit, they were off to the restaurant.

'Okay love, what's the surprise then?' she asked.

'Oh, it's nothing to get too excited about,' he replied, with a smile on his face.

Mum knew he was a teaser, and it was one of his most endearing features to her. They arrived at the restaurant, and he led her to a table where there was a bunch of roses and a candle already lit.

Mum's eyes lit up. The smile on her face made Dad instinctively kiss her on the cheek.

'Let me take your coat, madam,' said the waiter. 'Please sit, and I will bring the menus.'

After the waiter had brought their drinks and taken their order, Dad decided that she had waited long enough.

'Okay love,' he said, 'hold out your hands and close your eyes.'

Mum did as she was told. She was feeling really excited as he placed the envelope in her hands.

'Okay, you can open your eyes now,' he said in a loving tone.

Mum was bewildered. She still could not work out what it was.

'Is it a cheque from the football pools?' she said with a smile.

'Open it and see,' Dad replied with a huge grin, hoping she was going to be as happy about this as he was.

Mum's eyes filled with tears of joy as she looked up at him. She was speechless and for a few seconds was in shock. She got up and went round to Dad's side of the table and threw her arms around him.

'I love you so much, Pat,' she said, as the tears streaked down the faces of them both.

Although Mum was overjoyed that she had her birth certificate and now knew her real mother's name, she was slightly upset that her name on the birth certificate had never been used.

The name on the certificate was Sally, and she was puzzled why she was known as Rose – not that she didn't like the name, but she didn't understand why she wasn't known as Sally. It was not something she was going to worry about, and she decided that if the opportunity to find out came up, then so be it, but if not, she would just forget it.

Mum's real mother's address was on the birth certificate and she was so happy that she now knew her name.

'Grace is such a lovely name,' she said to Dad. 'And just to think that she lived in London! I wonder if she still lives there.'

She was starting to feel excited, but Dad knew there was much more work to do, and that there was a possibility that he might not find Mum's natural mother but he would do everything in his power to make it happen.

Mum was more optimistic.

'Let's think positive,' she said. 'And I promise not to get my hopes up too much.'

They enjoyed the rest of the meal, and chatted generally about us kids and how delighted they were now that she was home for good. They both left the restaurant feeling very happy.

Over the next few weeks Mum's demeanour improved. It was clear that obtaining her birth certificate had had a positive effect on her. Dad knew he would have to plan the next stage, and asked Aunty Victoria if she would help. She was between jobs, and Dad knew she would enjoy getting involved in finding Grace.

He gave her Grace's address and maiden name at the time of Mum's birth, and a letter for Grace that he had written on the off chance that Victoria was successful.

Victoria decided to take the bus for the thirty-mile trip to East London, where Grace had been living when she had given birth to Mum. Dad had wondered whether the address on the birth certificate was correct or whether it had been false. It wasn't that he was cynical, but he thought of everything. He also wondered whether the correct names had been filled in, but there was only one way to find out and he was determined.

Victoria arrived in London at around 10:00am, and made her way to the address on the birth certificate by taxi. Despite being a very confident woman, she found that she was very nervous when she approached the front door of the little terraced house.

She knocked on the door. After waiting for what seemed like several minutes she knew that whoever lived there was not at home. She decided to knock on the neighbour's door. An elderly woman opened it, and Victoria started on the well-rehearsed lines that she had planned for this eventuality.

'Hello I wonder if you can help me. I am trying to find a distant relative who lived next door in 1941. I know it's a long shot, but her name is Grace.'

Aunty Victoria had a nice way about her and the elderly woman could see that she was genuine.

'Well,' she said, 'I have lived here since 1936, and I don't recall a Grace living there, but Alice, the lady who used to live there, had a granddaughter called Grace. She was a beautiful young lady, always polite, and she visited her grandmother quite often.'

Victoria could feel her adrenaline rise.

'Alice died about twenty years ago,' said the woman. 'I don't know what happened to Grace – I never saw her after that. You could ask Dolly, who lives at number twenty-six – she and Grace were good friends.'

Victoria thanked her and made her way to number twenty-six, praying that Dolly would be in. She knocked on the door. When the door opened she explained who she was and that her neighbour a few doors away had told her she might be able to help.

'Come in, dear,' said Dolly. 'Would you like a cup of tea?'

Victoria's mouth was dry and she welcomed the offer.

'So how do you know Grace, then?' said Dolly.

Victoria had concocted a story that she was a distant cousin and was working on her family tree.

'I'm trying to piece together my family history,' she said. 'Grace is a second cousin. I'd love to find her and see if I can arrange a family reunion.'

Dolly found the story completely credible. Although Victoria wasn't comfortable about not telling her the full truth, she knew that she had to try to find out whether Dolly knew that Grace had had a child in 1941.

After they had chatted for some time it was clear that Dolly didn't know where Grace lived now, or that Grace had given birth in 1941.

'As far as I know, Grace's mother lives in a small block of flats about two miles away.'

Dolly had visited the flat with Alice on a few occasions, and was able to give Victoria information enough for her to find the flats, though Dolly didn't know the number of the flat itself.

14

GIVING GRACE THE NEWS

Victoria was tired, and decided to make her way back home to report back to Dad and plan another visit to London to follow up her new-found information, despite the urge to keep going.

She was ecstatic at what she had discovered, and had promised to keep in touch with Dolly and let her know how she got on with her enquiries. She was looking forward to getting home and seeing Dad to let him know that she had made contact with people who knew Grace.

Victoria knew that if she did manage to find Grace, it would come as a total shock to her that her firstborn was trying to find her, but she knew that she had to find out Grace's circumstances before giving Grace the news.

That evening she phoned Dad and asked him whether he could pop over. Mum knew nothing of their plan, as they didn't want her to get her hopes up at this stage. After explaining to Dad the events of the day, she told him she would go back to London the following week and follow up on the information she had gained. Dad was excited, but despite wanting to tell Mum, he decided that, for now, it would be better to be patient and let Victoria take control.

When Victoria went back to London, she arrived at the block of flats that Dolly had told her about, and was determined to knock on every door if need be.

After speaking to most of the people in the flats and failing to find out any further information, she felt very deflated. She decided to call in at a local café for a cup of tea and think of her next plan of action. The café was very busy, and Victoria sat down at a table with two other middle-aged women.

'Hello dear, you look troubled,' said one of them.

'Oh, hello. It's nothing, really. I'm just tired and a bit frustrated.'

Victoria was very sociable and briefly told the lady about her plight. She was surprised when the woman said she thought she knew who Victoria was talking about. The woman was sure that the Grace that Victoria was referring to was a popular woman who had lived in the area for years and was now living in a new block of flats close by. She wasn't totally sure, but it was a close neighbourhood, and she told Victoria that it was worth her finding out who she was.

Victoria couldn't believe her luck. Could this really be Grace? She was given the name of two blocks to try, and was told that if it was the Grace that she was looking for, most people would know her.

She finished her tea and, after thanking the woman, made her way to the blocks of flats, where she proceeded to knock on doors and ask anyone who answered whether they knew anyone called Grace and explained that she was a distant relative.

Eventually a woman in one of the blocks told her that there was someone called Grace who lived on the third floor, but that she was not sure what number.

Victoria soon established the correct flat, and approached the front door. She knocked, and could see through the glass pane that someone was coming to answer the door.

Victoria was very nervous now. She prayed that it was Grace, but knew that she had to be very discreet with what she said.

'Hello' said a woman as she opened the door.

'Hello' said Victoria. 'You don't know me, but I hope you can help me. Is your husband at home?'

'No, he's at work at the moment,' Grace said.

Victoria could see the likeness and was fairly sure that she had found Mum's real mother.

'My name is Victoria, and I have a very sensitive question to ask you.'

Grace was confused, but, having had three children and a husband who was a bit of a rogue, she naturally assumed that one of them might be in trouble.

'May I come in, please?' said Victoria.

'It depends what you want,' replied Grace.

'It's about Sally,' said Victoria, looking Grace directly in the eye.

'What about Sally?' said Grace, in an almost unconcerned tone of voice. 'Is she in trouble? Has she had an accident?'

Victoria was confused.

'Who do you think I am talking about?' she said, puzzled.

'You just told me – Sally, my daughter.'

It suddenly dawned on Grace that Victoria was talking about her first child.

'Come in, come in,' she said, looking up and down the landing to see if there were any neighbours about.

'I'm so sorry, Victoria, but I was confused. One of my daughters' name is Sally. I called her that because I never thought I would see my first daughter again. But who are *you*?'

'I am Sally's sister-in-law, Victoria. I've managed to track you down through Sally's birth certificate.'

Grace had to sit down and collect her thoughts for a moment,

'How did you find me? How is Sally? Where is she?' Grace was shocked. She had never expected this day to come, though secretly she often thought about her first daughter and wondered how she was, whether she was married, or whether she had any children.

'Sally is fine, and happily married with four children,' Victoria told her.

At this news Grace broke down in floods of tears. Immediately Victoria comforted her. Victoria had known the shock would be intense, and she too felt very emotional.

'I will make us a cup of tea,' said Grace, composing herself.

'You know I am married now and have three children don't you?' she went on.

'No, I know nothing about you,' said Victoria, 'and Sally doesn't even know that I am here. She has been ill, and although she is getting better she desperately wants to know who her real mother is.'

Grace had never told her husband or her children that she had had a baby in 1941. To tell them now would devastate them, as she had always been honest and had brought the children up to be honest.

Victoria told Grace as much as she could about Mum's life, and how she was now known as Rose, but she didn't go into too much detail about what had happened to her as a child as she knew that it could cause Grace unnecessary guilt.

She gave Grace the letter that Dad had written. Grace promised that she would write to Mum to explain that while she was happy to meet her, she could not tell her own family that she had another daughter.

After Victoria and Grace had exchanged telephone numbers and said their goodbyes, Grace closed the door and sat down with the letter that Dad had written, nervous about what she would read.

Tears filled her eyes as she opened the letter and saw a photo of Mum with Dad, Elizabeth, the boys and me. She read the letter, which hinted that Mum's life had been anything but normal. Dad had tried to be as subtle as he could, and had taken care to give enough detail for Grace to know that Mum did not blame her for anything.

But time was getting on, and Grace's husband, Tom, and her youngest daughter, Jenny, were due home. She knew that they would suspect something if she didn't freshen up and act normal. Grace hid the letter and photo, but knew that she would look at the photo at every opportunity when she was alone.

When Victoria had returned from meeting Grace a few days earlier, she relayed all of the information to Dad, and although he was disappointed, he was satisfied that they had done all they could. He was worried how Mum would take the news, as he knew she would want to rush up to London and meet her real Mother for the first time.

He chose a moment when Mum was in a particularly buoyant mood to tell her the news.

'Darling, I have some news about your real Mum,' he said in a happy tone.

Mum stopped what she was doing and focused on his words.

'What about her?' she said.

'Well, it's good news, but we have to take things slowly, that's all.'

He went on to explain the situation, and was relieved that Mum understood. He told her that she should be receiving a letter from her mum any day.

Mum knew what time the postman arrived, and would be waiting for him to come up the road in the mornings, but after five days without a letter, she started to think the worst and that her Mum didn't want to know her.

On the sixth day after Victoria had located Mum's mother, and when Mum least expected it, a letter arrived by the afternoon delivery. She could see by the postmark that it was from London, and hoped desperately that it was from her mum.

She opened the letter carefully, as she did all letters, and wept with mixed delight and sadness at what her Mum had written.

'To my darling daughter,

I would like to tell you straight away that I never stopped thinking about you, and there were many times when I wished that I had not had to have you adopted. I am so sorry, Rose, but my reasons were that I was only seventeen and our house was very small, just a two-up, two-down terraced house which was home to eight people. My father was a strict man, and if he had found out I was pregnant there was a strong chance he would have made me have an abortion, and I couldn't do that. It was very difficult for me to keep my pregnancy a secret and the only person who knew was my nan, who made all the arrangements for me to have you safely and to arrange for your future welfare. Pat's letter suggested that your adoptive parents weren't very nice towards you, and I hope that it wasn't all bad. I do feel guilty about not being there for you, but my life was very difficult when I got pregnant and I just wanted what was best for you.

I had only known your father a short while, and when he found out I was pregnant he was off like a shot. He was a nice person, but didn't want the responsibility of being a father. We had not planned to have a baby, but you know how these things can happen.

I can tell you that you have two sisters and a brother. Sally is thirty, Patrick is twenty-five and Jenny is nearly twenty. Jenny has a baby who has just turned three, so I am often called on to babysit. My husband, Tom, is a lovely man. He is a bit of a rogue, but everybody loves him and he is very popular where we live. I have thought about telling him about you, but I know it would break his heart to know that I had had a baby before we got married. He is a very old-fashioned man, and he thinks he was my first love. I hope you can forgive me, but I just can't tell him at the moment. If you are happy to meet up some time in the future, I am sure we can arrange it, but I don't want to raise suspicion, so it would mean that you would have to come to London, as it would be difficult for me to disappear for hours on end. Anyway, my darling daughter, I am so glad that you have a beautiful family, and I am sure we will all meet up one day and get to know each other. I will write to you again soon, but for now take care of yourself and the children and say hello to Pat and Victoria for me.

All my love,

Mum xxx'

To have a letter from her real mother, signed '*All my love, Mum xxx*' meant everything to Mum. Her adoptive mother had never signed off a birthday card, Christmas card or any other letter or card with the words '*All my love, Mum xxx*'

After she had read the letter she went to the bureau to get a pen and paper to write her Mum a reply letter.

It wasn't until this point that she realized that her mother's letter had no forwarding address. She turned the letter over and over again, and even checked the envelope but there was no address or phone number. She was devastated, and burst into tears.

After an hour or so, and having composed herself, she decided to call Victoria and tell her about the letter she had received.

'Hello Victoria, it's Rose,' she said calmly. 'I've had a letter from my real Mum, but she forgot to put her address on the letter, could you let me have it please?'

Victoria felt very awkward, she knew that she could not divulge the address.

She knew that Mum wouldn't go racing up to London, but if she had written a letter and it was opened or even found by one of Grace's family it could cause serious problems for Grace.

'Oh, Rose, you know that's difficult for me. You do know that your Mum's husband and children don't know about you, don't you?'

There was silence for about ten seconds.

'I'll contact her and ask if she is happy for you to send a letter to her flat, and if not, whether she can provide an address that you can send a letter to.'

Mum trusted Victoria, and understood that she had to wait for her mum to come back with a decision.

Victoria called Grace and explained things to her, and Grace provided an address for Mum to send a letter to.

Grace had a long-term friend, and although she had known nothing about Grace having had a baby, she was glad to help and understood the sensitivity of the situation.

Victoria phoned Mum and gave her the details. Mum was overjoyed at the news, and sent the letter off with more photographs of us all in the hope that her Mum would want to meet us. For the next year or so, letters were exchanged every two months or so.

Although Mum suggested meeting up, there were always reasons why this could not happen. But Mum was content, and the communication helped with her state of mind.

One sunny morning a letter arrived in the first post, and Mum instantly recognized the handwriting. She sat down to read the letter over a cup of tea.

She could hardly believe what she was reading, and tears filled her eyes as she realised that she was going to meet her Mum for the first time. The letter she had received was tinged with sadness, but it did mean that her life was about to change, and she realized that what it contained must have been very difficult for her Mum to write, in particular the part about her husband, Tom.

To my darling daughter,

It is possible for us to meet up now, as my life has changed for ever. My darling husband Tom died recently from a heart attack, which has made me realize how important it is to make the most of our loved ones. I have told my children about you, and have shown them all of the photos you have sent me. After the initial shock they soon realized how important you are to me, and they are very supportive and excited about meeting their sister. Sally and Jenny in particular can't wait to meet you, and they look so much like you. I have included my phone number at the top of the letter. Call me on Saturday evening and we can arrange when to meet up. I look forward to meeting you and Pat, and my grandchildren too.

Take care, my darling Rose.

Love from Mum, xxx'

15

SOMETHING VERY SPECIAL

With the news that she was to meet her real mum and her siblings, Mum decided to cut ties completely with her adoptive parents, the people that I had known as Nan and Granddad.

Since the day when Elizabeth made that fateful visit, none of us had been round although we had spoken to Nan on the phone. Mum discussed it at length with Dad, who was in full support. Although the thought of never seeing Hugh again didn't trouble her one bit, she couldn't help feeling sorry for her adoptive mother Avril.

Mum had had no family members to talk to when she was young, and though she did re-establish relations with Violet and Joe – the parents of her first adoptive father – John, they had died some years ago.

She had tried to confide to Avril what was happening to her when she was young, especially when Hugh had started to sexually abuse her. Avril had done nothing to stop the abuse, and only accused Mum of lying or imagining what was happening to her.

Mum found it difficult, but she wrote a letter to Avril to explain the situation. She apologized for her decision, but she knew that it was the best course of action, as she had never felt true love for Avril, and until she met my dad, she had never experienced love at all.

It was time to tell us all about the past, and to explain that we would not be seeing our grandparents again. We had not had a great deal of contact with them, but as far as us boys knew, Avril and Hugh were Mum's parents and were therefore our grandparents. Elizabeth had been told all there was to know, so she had not seen Avril and Hugh for several years. But the news came as a shock to John and David and in particular to me.

I was now approaching twenty-one, and despite my short stature I was tough when it came to anyone hurting people that I love and care for.

'That's it! I'm going make him pay,' I told Mum and Dad.

'Don't you think *I've* wanted to hurt him, all these years?' said Dad. 'I have sat outside his house on several occasions, considering whether to go in and kill him, but that's not what Mum wants.'

He was trying to lead by example, and I knew that it must have been difficult for him not to take revenge, as he was not a man who would stand by and do nothing if he knew that anyone had harmed any members of our family.

'Mum just wants to put all that behind her and move on, so we have to respect her wishes and enjoy the fact that she is getting better now, and is going to meet her real Mum.'

I said that I would support whatever Mum wanted and leave it at that, but I knew I would not be able to ignore what Hugh had done. I needed to talk to Elizabeth. She was living with a friend and I decided to go and see her.

'Why didn't you tell me?' I said as Elizabeth opened the door. I was angry. I had felt that our relationship was close enough for us to share important secrets.

'Rick, I didn't tell you because Mum asked me not to, and if I *had* told you, I think you would have done something stupid.'

It had been hard for her to keep that secret for so long, as we were very close. She had sometimes come very close to telling me the truth, especially whenever I'd said that I was going to visit Nan and Granddad.

'You're bloody right: I *would* have done something,' I told her. 'He is going to pay for what he did to Mum, I swear.'

Elizabeth allowed me to rant and rave about our so-called grandparents until I had calmed down. I left after we had had a cup of tea and discussed how much better Mum was now, and how we were looking forward to meeting our real nan, aunts and uncles.

The following day, Elizabeth told Dad that I had been to see her and that I had threatened to make Hugh pay for what he had done to our Mum, and that she was worried that I might get in trouble.

'Don't worry, love, I'll have a word with him. Things will be okay, you'll see. He's just angry, that's all.'

Later that day, Dad and I went to a café at lunchtime to talk things through.

'Dad, I'm telling you now, he's going to pay for what he has done.'

Dad knew how angry I was, he too had felt the same way when he first found out.

'Please listen to what I am saying, son. If your Mum thought you were going to do something, it would worry her, and you know how that would affect her, so let's try to move on and respect her wishes, eh?' Dad knew it would be hard for me to forget it, but he was sure it was just the initial anger that was making me say these things.

'Okay Dad, I will try, but I just hope I don't bump into him, as I don't think I will be able to stop myself from doing something.'

While we ate our lunch, I was already planning some nasty things to do to Hugh in my head. I was certain I would carry them out.

We finished our lunch in silence and went back to work.

Mum was looking forward to phoning her Mum on Saturday evening, and was counting down the hours.

'What time do you think I should call?' she asked Dad.

'I'd say six o'clock would be the best time,' he said.

He knew that Mum was excited about phoning her Mum. She would have phoned at three o'clock if she could.

At five to six Mum couldn't wait any longer, and picked up the receiver.

Dad had asked her if she wanted to be alone, but she told him she wanted him there, and that he should speak to her too, as he was more familiar with London and would have to take the directions for when they would go and meet her.

Mum also knew that he was excited too, and if it hadn't been for him she would never have been in a position to receive letters from her Mum, let alone be arranging to meet her.

Elizabeth and I knew about the phone call and had decided to be there when Mum phoned. We were sitting behind the top landing banisters out of sight, but we knew we would be able to hear one half of the conversation.

'Hello it's Rose here,' Mum said as her mother answered the phone. She hadn't given her a chance to say anything, such was her eagerness to speak to her.

'Hello Rose, my darling. How are you?'

Mum had a lump in her throat, and it was a few seconds before she could answer.

'I'm fine now, but I do feel a bit emotional, and I'm not sure what to call you. It feels odd, calling you "Mum".'

'Well, my darling, I *am* your mum, and I want you to call me that. It was hard for *me* to call you Rose in the letters that I wrote, as *I* always knew you as Sally. But I am used to it now and you will soon get used to calling me Mum.'

If Mum was nervous, Grace was just as nervous, but their conversation soon made them both feel at ease. After they had talked for an hour about their families and how much they were looking forward to meeting, it was left to Dad to introduce himself and get the details of where they were going to meet.

Grace had decided that their first meeting should be somewhere neutral, and suggested a small park close to where she lived. She asked Dad to bring all the children and Victoria too.

Dad handed the phone back to Mum. After they arranged to meet on the following Saturday at three o'clock they said their goodbyes and hung up.

Mum felt elated, but emotionally drained. As she looked into Dad's eyes she threw her arms around him and burst into tears.

'I love you so much, Pat. You made this happen. I don't know how long it took you, or what you had to do, but I am sure it wasn't easy.'

He held her tight. He could feel the tears running down her check and onto his neck. This made his own eyes fill up, but he managed to hold himself together. Dad found it difficult to show his emotions, but they were always close to the surface at times like this.

'I love you, too,' he said, 'and I'm going to plan a celebration party for two weeks' time. Maybe your mum and her family will come.'

Mum eventually let go of Dad, although she could have held him for the rest of the evening.

Elizabeth and I looked at each other and knew this was the start of something new and exciting for us all. We couldn't wait to meet our real nan.

Mum and Dad loved each other so much, and after all they had been through, they both knew that this marked the start of something very special for us all too. Mum's demeanour changed overnight, and she could be found singing and humming, whatever she was doing. Speaking to her Mum had such a dramatic effect on her that everyone noticed.

Once she had been nervous about going out, and had to force herself to go to the local shop. Now she was eager to get out and tell people her news.

As the weekend approached Mum met up with Victoria and asked her for advice about what she should wear and what she should ask. She wasn't exactly nervous about seeing her Mum for the first time, but the excitement of it was overwhelming her.

Saturday finally arrived and we set off in two cars. Dad led the way in his car with Mum and Victoria. and I followed in my car with Elizabeth, John and David. We were all excited at the prospect of meeting our new nan.

When we pulled up at the small park next to the block of flats where Nan lived, though we didn't know it, she was watching us from the balcony of her flat. Once she was sure it was us, she made her way down.

'She'll be here in a minute,' said Mum confidently.

We walked into the little park. Dad, Mum and Victoria sat on a bench while Elizabeth stood next to Mum and held her hand. John and David sat on the ground and chatted generally while I looked around for signs of a middle-aged woman.

At last, after a couple of minutes, someone emerged from the block of flats. It was clear, as she headed towards the little park, that it was our nan. As Victoria had previously met her, she got up from the bench and opened the small gate for her.

'Hello Victoria! Lovely to see you again,' said Nan, giving her a kiss on the cheek.

Mum walked towards her mum. As they approached each other, they were both speechless and rushed over the last few feet before throwing their arms round each other.

'Oh, Mum! I can't believe it,' said Mum in her mother's ear. 'I've waited all my life for this moment, I've never felt so happy.'

Nan held Mum tight and it was some time before either of them could compose themselves. We all had tears in our eyes, and to see Mum so happy was joyous.

'Hello Pat,' Nan said eventually. She and Mum had let go of each other, but were still holding hands.

Dad gave Nan a hug and kissed her cheek as if he had known her for years.

'Come and give your nan a kiss, then,' she said as she looked at us. We didn't need a second invitation; we hugged her one by one and instantly knew that she was a lovely, warm-hearted lady.

She had originally decided that we should just meet in the park the first time, as she had expected to be more emotional than in fact she was, and she didn't know how Mum was going to deal with it, but everything felt so natural, and she could feel the love between us all. So she invited us to her flat, and within just a few minutes we were stepping out of the lift.

'I'll just put the kettle on,' said Nan. 'Then I've just got to pop and see someone a few doors away.'

As she left the flat there was an air of mystery.

'Where has she gone?' John asked Mum.

'I'm not sure, love; she just said that she was popping out for a moment.'

A few minutes later the front door opened, and Nan walked in, followed by her daughter, Jenny, and her four-year-old granddaughter.

'Rose, this is your sister, Jenny, and my granddaughter, Marie.'

As Mum stood up she was shocked at the likeness between Jenny and her mum, and Jenny too was shocked at the likeness between Mum, her other sister, Sally as well as her own mother. It was uncanny. There was definitely no disputing that they were family.

After the initial introductions, Nan made tea and brought out some cakes and biscuits.

After two hours of pleasant chat and much laughter it was time for us to leave, but not before Dad had invited his new mother-in-law and her family to the party that he was planning in aid of the family reunion.

As we drove away and waved to Nan, Jenny and Marie, who were waving from the balcony, Mum couldn't help but shed a few tears of happiness and sheer joy.

The drive home was filled with talk about the party and who would be invited. We were all really looking forward to meeting her other sister, Sally, her brother, Patrick, and their children.

It had been clear that our two families were very similar and enjoyed partying and getting together on special occasions. The garden party was organised for two weeks time and the list of people invited had grown to over fifty. The weather forecast was good, and Dad prepared everything in his usual detailed way. Nothing was left to chance, and just in case the weather did change, he had set up a system whereby he could cover half the garden with a tarpaulin in just a few minutes.

Dad had also prepared banners with "WELCOME TO THE FAMILY" and "REUNITED FOREVER". Dad was pleased to hear that all of Nan's children would be coming, and that they would be bringing their children, who ranged from four to twelve. This was going to be a day to remember.

On the day of the party, Nan and her family arrived in three cars. There was a buzz of excitement among them as they knocked on our door. They had all been looking forward to meeting their new family member, and when Mum answered the door, the smile on her face made them all feel hugely welcome.

'Hello Mum,' she said, stepping forward to give Nan a kiss. 'Hi, Jenny, lovely to see you again,' and they hugged.

'This is Sally, and this is Patrick,' said Jenny as she introduced her, 'and this is John and Maria. Their other halves.'

'Come in,' said Mum as she gave them all a hug and kissed them on the cheek. They all came into the house and were led out to the back garden, where Dad and the rest of us were waiting to greet them.

It took a while for us all to greet each other, and there were far too many names for us all to remember. The atmosphere from the off was one of sheer excitement. Although Mum had been slightly worried about how her siblings would take to her, she had no reason to worry. There was an instant respect that would grow into brotherly and sisterly love in a very short space of time. We all felt relaxed in each other's company fairly quickly.

'Right. Who's going to help me put the tent up?' said Dad in a loud voice to the younger children. They all jumped up, and Dad took them to the bottom of the garden to help break the ice with them. He got them all working together to put up the four-berth tent, which he had already laid out by the back fence.

As Mum sat on one of the garden benches that Dad had set up, Elizabeth saw to the drinks and I took over from Dad to help the younger children to erect the tent.

It wasn't long before the tent was up and it became the den for all the younger children to play in. Before long they were giggling and laughing together as if they had known each other for years.

Nan was so happy – she had gone from having five grandchildren to having nine, and here we were all together. Not being able to meet her first born, or tell her husband about Mum had played on her conscience. That was all behind her now, and though she missed her husband greatly, she had a large and loving family who could keep her more than occupied.

The party was a huge success, and when it was time for Nan and her family to go home, plans were made for us all to meet up for a day at the seaside in a few weeks time. Mum assured them that a huge picnic would be planned, and that they would enjoy going out in the speedboat that Dad had built the year before.

The following six months saw us all get together often. Great times were had at the seaside, and also in Hackney, East London, at the local community club that Nan belonged to.

Before too long photo albums were filled with Mum, Nan and other family members, that captured the laughter and fun that had been missing from Mum's life for so long.

Mum went from strength to strength with her long-standing mental and emotional problems, and when she thought about it, she wondered how she could have let the voices in her head control her life in such a devastating way. Mum managed to control her demons, and as we grew up and started to become less reliant on her, she found that she enjoyed the garden more; and with the little Jack Russell that Dad had bought her for company, she was in her element.

Elizabeth and I would call in to see Mum regularly. Often, we would spend the evening playing cards and other board games with our parents and the boys. It would often be the early hours of the morning before we went home. John and David regularly had friends over and they would join in the games.

Mum looked forward to the card nights. She had a huge jar full of coins, and if any of the boys' friends came round she would share what she had in order for them to join in. If they lost the money it didn't matter to her, but if they won, she would only take back what she had given them. It was a fun house and Mum became very popular with the boys' friends.

'I wish *my* parents were like yours,' said one of John's friends one evening. 'All they want to do is sit and watch television.'

Dad and Mum looked at each other with a little smirk on their faces. They fully understood the sentiment behind the comment.

The change in both Mum and Dad was noticeable to everyone. Dad was very popular among my friends, as he was very witty, and many of them had said to me, 'I wish my dad was like your Dad.' It was his sense of humour and his sense of fun and adventure that made him stand out from the crowd.

Dad would often arrange weekends away with close friends and other family members. He knew how to rally people and encourage them to be more outgoing. Mum loved his character, and would support him in anything that he wanted to do; she knew he would always have other people's interests at heart. All he ever wanted to do was make people happy and make them laugh. It was something that Dad was very good at.

The following couple of years or so were filled with plenty of camping holidays, and it was not unusual for there to be a convoy of five or six cars travelling to our favourite camp site.

Mum was enjoying some of the best years of her life. It reminded her so much of when we were very young. Dad and I had a good working relationship, and would often have a pint on the way home from work. I really enjoyed Dad's company. We would sometimes meet up later in the evening at the local snooker club, although I would hardly ever win a game, when I did, it felt good. I looked up to Dad, and despite the problems of the past I was inspired by him, and often said to my friends, 'If ever I'm half the man my dad is, I will be a lucky man.'

Dad wasn't an angel, and if anything came along that was too cheap to say no to he would ask no questions and buy it, particularly if it was something for the home.

Mum was never too surprised when he walked in the door with the latest gadget, and if she even suggested that she wouldn't mind a new this or that, it was there shortly after. Dad wanted the best for Mum and although she never nagged him for anything, she knew she didn't have too. He was well aware of her needs.

Dad was doing everything he could for us all and he was enjoying seeing us grow up and go our own ways. He had always encouraged us to be self-sufficient and spread our wings, because he knew how important that freedom is to a young person.

Dad would still pick his mum up from where she lived at his brother's house every Tuesday and bring her home for dinner. One day when he arrived to pick her up, he was surprised to hear that she was not feeling too well.

'Okay Mum,' he said, 'not to worry. I'll pick you up next week.'

He stayed with her for a while and then came home.

A couple of hours later he had a telephone call from his brother, William, to tell him that their mum had been rushed into hospital with breathing problems.

Dad was worried, and drove straight to the hospital, where his brothers and sisters were waiting.

'Hello my name is Doctor James, I'm afraid the news is not good.'

They looked at each other and knew exactly what the next line would be. The doctor spoke at length about what had led to her death, but they were all too shocked to take it in.

The funeral was held a couple of weeks later, and the church was too small to cope with the large turnout.

She had had eight children and, at the time of her death, she had twenty-six grandchildren and ten great grandchildren.

The wake was held at a local hall that could accommodate our large family, and although it was a sad time, we raised our glasses to her and enjoyed the party atmosphere, which is what she would have wanted.

PART FOUR:

THE SEEDS OF REVENGE

16

THE FIRST ACT OF VENGEANCE

Three years after Mum had met her real mother, there had been many parties and family gatherings, and despite Mum's fortnightly injection for her paranoid schizophrenia, she was functioning well and enjoying life. Mum had maintained her happiness, partly due to advances in her medication and partly due to having built a strong relationship with her real mum and siblings. She did have the odd spell of mild depression, but she could recognize it and avoiding stressful situations soon brought her back to a good state of mind. On one of these occasions when she was feeling low, I paid her a visit and I was aware that she was not herself.

'What's up Mum?' I said, in an affectionate and supportive tone. We were very close and she loved it when I visited, as I would always give her a cuddle and make her laugh.

'Oh, it's nothing, love, I'm just feeling a bit low, that's all.'

I was determined to get to the bottom of why she was feeling low.

'Come on, Mum, you can tell me,' I said compassionately.

'Well, I have had a few flashbacks from when I was a girl, and it upsets me,' said Mum in a hushed voice. 'It will soon pass. Don't worry, love; I get it from time to time, but it doesn't last long.'

I knew exactly what those flashbacks were, and, after cheering Mum up with some funny stories, I left and decided to start acting on my plans to avenge the man who had caused her so much misery.

On my way home, I decided to drive past the house where Hugh and Avril lived, though I wasn't sure whether they still lived there, as there was no car on the driveway; and in any case they could well have changed it, I thought.

I parked, got out of my car and approached the front door of the house two doors away.

'Hello I wonder if you can help me,' I said, as a middle-aged woman opened the door. 'I'm trying to locate Mr and Mrs Harris. I have a parcel for them, but I'm not sure what number they live at as the address is torn, but it looks like no. 32. I did knock there but there was no answer.'

I showed no sign that I was lying, and the woman was very helpful.

'Yes, they do live at no. 32,' she said, looking out of the front door. She could see that their car wasn't on the driveway. 'It looks like they might be out at the moment,' she said cheerfully.

'Not to worry. I'm coming past tomorrow; I'll try then. Thank you for your help. Goodbye.'

I walked back to the car, excited to think that I could now start to torment the man who had made Mum's life so miserable. What he had done had affected all of our lives and I was looking forward to getting my own back.

I had never had a malicious way about me, but when anyone crossed me, I bided my time and got revenge when they had forgotten all about it, but this was on another level. I couldn't get the thoughts of avenging the person who I had once known as my granddad out of my mind, and I decided to start my campaign the following night.

I knew how much he loved his car – he always had the latest and most luxurious model he could afford. So damaging his car would infuriate him, but I would have to do it after dark and I would not be able to make too much noise. Putting fish down the front grille would not have been enough for this act of vengeance, so I soon came up with a new and much more costly act.

A year or so earlier, I had been carrying out some maintenance on my own car and left a tin of brake fluid on the roof. Once I was clearing up, I moved the tin and noticed that the paint had started to bubble up where a small amount of brake fluid had run down the side of the tin and onto the roof. I wiped it up quickly, but it was too late – a small section of the paint had been stripped.

When I asked a mechanic friend about this, it became clear that brake fluid was a good paint stripper if left for even a few minutes. So that was it: I knew what my first act was going to be. After work the following day, I stopped at a car accessories and parts shop and bought a medium-size tin of brake fluid.

Later that evening, just after dusk, I told Anne that I had to pop out and see someone about some work and would be back within the hour. I knew that, in order to use all of the brake fluid and to carry out my plan as quickly as possible, I would have to empty the fluid into a bigger container and throw it over the car rather than try to empty it out through the small opening in the tin.

I took with me a small paint kettle that I used at work. After I had driven past the property and found Hugh's car neatly parked on the driveway, I pulled up around the corner, took the brake fluid from the boot of my car and emptied it into the paint kettle.

I put the paint kettle into a bag, closed the boot and walked around the corner. Although I felt a little nervous, I was determined to carry out the first of my plans this night. As I walked down the road, I looked to any unsuspecting person like a young man returning from the local shop.

I walked past the property and cautiously looked around to ensure that the curtains were closed in the house and the immediate neighbours. Satisfied that all was clear, I turned around and walked back up the road. As soon as I got to Hugh's car I reached into the bag and pulled out the paint kettle. Within two seconds, I had poured all of the brake fluid over the bonnet of Hugh's shiny new car. I put the paint kettle back in the bag, took a surreptitious look around me and walked calmly on.

When I got back to my car, all was quiet. I put the bag on the passenger side foot well and drove off. My heart was pounding more than I had expected, but I felt good. I knew that my actions would cause distress to Hugh, and I would have given anything to be able to see his face the following morning.

Much as I wanted to tell Anne what I had done, I also knew that she would not have approved. It was going to be a long, sustained campaign and I couldn't risk anyone finding out. The only person that I knew I could confide in was my best friend, Stan.

I met Stan at the age of eleven when we started at the same high school together. He moved from South London to the seaside town where I grew up in Essex. With his flat nose, he looked like someone who could look after himself in a scrap. It turned out that he was a schoolboy amateur boxer, and a good one at that. It wasn't too long before we were both boxing at the same club and that's where our close friendship started.

Stan and I often worked together as our paths crossed in the self-employed building world. I had always looked up to him, he was tough in body and in mind and, although I didn't know it at the time, Stan thought the same about me.

I had told Stan what had happened to my mum and that I would get even with Hugh some day.

The following day I called round to see Stan, and asked him if he would drive by Hugh's house and see whether the car was still there and how bad the damage was. Stan was more than happy to help and, after returning home, he told me that Hugh's car was not there.

We discussed how seriously the brake fluid would have damaged the car, and were sure that it would have necessitated a full re-spray. Between the two of us, we came up with a variety of things to do over the next few years to torment Hugh. After all, as I told Stan, 'What Hugh did to my mum from the age of three to the age of sixteen is not going to go unpunished.' Stan was reliable and I could trust him one hundred per cent not to say anything to anyone.

Three days after I had carried out my first act of vengeance, I arrived home at the usual time, and sat down to read the local paper while Anne was preparing the dinner. I always bought the local paper on the way home as I often had advertisements in it for my services as a local builder, and I was always interested in who the competition was.

As I was flicking through the paper I spotted a headline reading 'CAR VANDALISED BY LOCAL YOBS'. As I started to read the article it was clear that it related to what I had done. I was pleased to read that Hugh had only just bought the car and that it would require a full re-spray. It went on to say that Mr Harris had no idea who would want to damage his car and that it was inconveniencing him, as it would be three weeks before he would get it back.

After dinner I decided to visit Stan. I was eager to show Stan the article, and took the local paper with me, I told Anne that I wanted to show Stan a couple of cheap cars that were being advertised.

'Nice one, mate,' said Stan when he read the paper. 'There will be more articles like this before we're finished.'

I was glad to be able to confide in Stan. It was important for me to have somebody who understood my reasons for avenging Mum's tormentor and abuser.

17

THE NEWS

'Hi, Mum,' I said one day as Mum answered the phone.

'Hello love. How are you?'

'Oh, I'm not bad, Mum but Anne's not too good.'

Mum was instantly concerned.

'Oh, why's that love? Nothing serious, I hope.'

I always teased Mum, and although I didn't want to worry her, I wanted to make an impact with the news that I was about to give her. I made a point of not sounding too concerned.

'No, she's well enough, but she's put on quite lot of weight just lately, and she's getting bigger by the week.'

'Well, she looked fine to me the other day,' said Mum, trying to give me some assurance.

'Yeah, I'm sure she'll be fine Mum, but the doctor wants to see her regularly until she has the baby.'

Mum was speechless.

'What did you say?' she blurted out after a few seconds.

'Your going to be a nan in July, Mum.'

I knew Mum would be excited by the news, so when I heard her sobbing down the phone, I wished I had driven round and told her face to face.

'Mum, are you all right?' I said, concerned.

'Oh, Rick!' she said through her sobs. 'I am so happy for you and Anne. I'm just overwhelmed at the moment. Let me phone you back in a while.'

I wished I hadn't played the trick on her, and I told her that I would pop round and see her straight away.

When Anne and I arrived twenty minutes later, Mum was waiting at the window and answered the door before we had time to knock.

'Hello Nan!' I said with a big smile on my face. We all hugged and enjoyed the moment.

'Now then, Anne,' said Mum, 'if you need anything at all, you just let me know.' She was so excited that she wanted to start getting ready for her role as a nan.

We waited for Dad to get in, and he, too, was pleased that he was going to be a granddad. He knew that Mum would be very excited and would do whatever she could to help us prepare for the big day.

Although Mum was now considerably better than she had been for years, the experiences that she had been through had left their mark. She now recognized good times and would make the most of them.

Now, at the age of forty-one, she was going to be a grandmother, and it was the best news that she had had for years. Mum loved babies, and on her trips to the local shops she would always stop and chat to young mothers who had toddlers or babies in prams.

She couldn't wait to tell everyone, and as soon as we had left, she phoned around the family to let them know the good news, and the first person she called was her mum.

Nan was overjoyed at the news that she was going to be a great-grandmother and asked Mum to pass on her best wishes. Anne's parents were equally happy about the news, and, being slightly more old-fashioned than my mum and dad, her Mum had suggested to Anne that she should get married before the baby was born.

We were finding things hard financially, but with contributions from both sets of parents we were married when Anne was four months pregnant.

Mum and Dad visited us shortly before Anne was due to give birth, and they had a surprise for us. I was self-employed, and although I was hardly ever out of work, times were tough, and any help was always welcome.

'Hi, love,' said Mum as Anne opened the door.

'Hello Rose! Hi, Pat!' she said in a happy voice.

'How's the bump?' said Mum joyfully.

'Oh, it's getting bigger, and I can't wait to have the baby,' said Anne.

It was June, and the weather was extremely warm, which Anne found hard to cope with.

I made the tea, and we all sat down and chatted about the forthcoming birth and baby names. Just as Mum and Dad had decided not to know the sex of their unborn children, we had decided to wait until our baby was born.

Mum put a bag on the table, which Anne opened.

'There you go, Anne, I have put a few things together for you.'

Anne pulled out the items one by one and was delighted with what Mum had put in the bag: crocheted blankets of neutral colours, baby-grows, bottles and various powders and creams.

'Thanks Rose. You shouldn't have done that,' said Anne politely.

'Don't be so daft; it's the least I can do,' said Mum. She wanted to do more, but was conscious that Anne's parents and many other people would also be buying little presents.

Throughout Anne's pregnancy, all members of the family and their extended families made up little gift packs to show their happiness for us. Mum telephoned everyone in her little address book, she was so excited at the prospect of being a Nan.

The day arrived in early July for Anne to have the baby. I took her to the hospital at midnight when her contractions had started to increase. I had phoned Mum earlier that evening to tell her that Anne's waters had broken and that it was likely she would have the baby that night.

I needed to hear Mum's voice to reassure and advise me, as I wasn't sure when I should take Anne to the hospital, but, when the time came, Anne knew when she needed to go, and reassured me. I was really excited about becoming a Dad.

Anne's contractions lasted throughout the night and into the following morning, and I was by her bedside all night. I telephoned Mum and Anne's parents in the morning to keep them updated, and promised to phone them with any news later on.

Anne was struggling with her contractions, which were now becoming very painful. By midday, the midwife was concerned, but she wanted Anne to have the baby naturally rather have to undergo a surgical birth.

Gas and air were administered and by two o'clock in the afternoon the baby was close to being born. I was still by Anne's side and trying to reassure her during her painful contractions.

Eventually the midwife told me that the baby's head was showing, and in the next moment, the head was fully out.

'I can see the baby's head,' I said excitedly.

'Is it a boy or girl?' said Anne.

'I don't know if it's a boy or girl yet, but it hasn't got a moustache, so it could be a girl,' I replied.

The baby was born at ten minutes past two, and it was a boy.

'What's the time?' asked Anne.

'Its ten past two,' replied the nurse.

'Oh, I hope he hasn't got ten-to-two feet, like Charlie Chaplin!' said Anne.

The gas and air had reduced Anne's pain threshold, but had made her slightly confused, and her comments made me laugh. The midwife and maternity staff found this extremely funny, and were happy that Anne had finally given birth to her baby naturally.

As Anne held the baby on her chest, she looked up at me and passed me the baby with the nurse's help. With tears of joy running down my face I told Anne, 'This is the best day of my life. I love you so much.'

I handed the baby back to the nurse who had to clean him up and complete the paperwork. Anne was shattered. The nurse told me that Anne and the baby both needed to have a few hours' rest before any visitors would be allowed in.

I went straight out to the local phone box and called my mum and my in-laws to tell them the good news.

'So what are you going to call him, then?' said Mum.

'I don't know yet, Mum. We have a couple of names to choose from, but until Anne has recovered I can't say, just in case she has decided on something different.'

We had provisionally agreed on the name Matthew, and when I visited Anne later that evening she was happy to keep to that. I again made the necessary calls to inform everyone, and over the next week Anne was visited in hospital by both sets of parents and was showered with presents for the baby.

*

As we adjusted to parenthood, we soon realized that Matthew was not going to give us much peace at night. After nine months of sleepless nights we decided that the only way to get Matthew to sleep was for him to cry himself to sleep. We tried for a few nights, but Matthew was getting himself into such a state of uncontrollable sobbing that Anne could not stand to listen to it, and wanted to have him in bed with us. I was happy to support her, as I didn't like Matthew suffering in that way either.

During all these times of happiness, I never let go of the thoughts of what Hugh had done to my Mum and continued my occasional acts of vengeance. I slashed Hugh's tyres and tipped boxes of nails and screws in his driveway every few months. I became very quick under the cover of darkness, and never once did I feel guilty.

We had planned to have another baby, as we wanted our children to grow up together, and were hoping that the next baby would be a girl. Anne fell pregnant again, and seventeen months after Matthew was born she gave birth once again in the same ward. It was midwinter now; the baby was born in the first week in January. It was a much less complicated birth for Anne this time, and we were delighted that it was a girl.

Anne was home with our new baby Marie after just a few days in the hospital, and we soon settled down to the challenges ahead of us. Matthew was still waking up during the night, and I would often have to get up and play with him at three or four o'clock in the morning, as his crying would wake Marie who was thankfully sleeping through the night at two months old.

We both found the first two years of Matthew's life very draining, though we coped with it well and eventually he started to sleep throughout the night. On the first couple of nights when Matthew started to sleep through, we would wake up and check that everything was okay. It was so unusual that it worried us at first – we thought that he had stopped breathing.

Six months after Marie was born, Elizabeth had a baby girl, who she named Jackie, and eighteen months after that she had a boy called Rob. We would often visit our parents, and Mum looked forward to seeing the grandchildren. She would always have something for them and loved to babysit.

Dad had built a huge pergola in the garden for her to grow plants and vines up and hang her flower baskets from. During the warm summer months we all got together in Mum's garden, where we would have barbecues and she would lay on a huge salad buffet. Dad and Mum would spend all afternoon playing in the garden with the grandchildren. David, John Elizabeth and myself were all very musical and would play our guitars and sing songs. These were some of the best times of Mum's life, and as usual, times like these were always captured on photographs.

Matthew, Marie, Jackie and Rob got on really well together, and as there were only five years between the eldest and the youngest, and as me and my sister lived fairly close to one and other, the kids bonded well. Anne and Elizabeth would often get together during the days and take the children to the park or down to the beach.

During the next couple of years, as the children grew, I spent more time with Mum and Dad. Although Mum didn't seem to show any signs of her previous depression or illness, I would often catch her staring and looking dazed.

'Are you all right, Mum?' I asked her one day when I had caught her in a mesmerised state.

'Oh, sorry, love,' said Mum. 'I was just thinking.'

I remembered how, some years ago, she would sometimes look as though she had horrible thoughts going on in her head, and was worried that she was beginning to dwell on her childhood days again.

'Well, Mum, as long as you're thinking good things, that's okay,' was all that I dared say.

John and David had moved out of the family home within the last couple of years, and I did wonder if she was just feeling a little lonely at times.

I had been preoccupied for a few years with being a dad and my plans to make Hugh pay had taken a back seat, although I knew he would certainly get what was coming to him when the moment was right.

By now, I was sure that my mum was still being troubled by her past. Although she loved seeing the grandchildren and spending time with them, and making them laugh and cuddling them when they got tired, I wondered whether this brought back memories of her own childhood and how she wished it had been like this. I decided to restart my campaign of vengeance, and made enquiries to find out whether Hugh and Avril still lived in the same house. I was happy to learn that they did. I drove past and saw that Hugh had a different car; it was nearly new and shining like a new pin, as his cars always were.

18

VIOLENT REVENGE

I called round to see Stan, who was always up for avenging anyone who had brought pain or heartache on anyone who was vulnerable and couldn't protect themselves. Together we decided to plan more attacks. We were not trying to upset Avril so much, but as far as I was concerned she was partly responsible for allowing Hugh to carry out his evil acts.

Hugh's house had windows with diagonal leaded panes. I knew that getting them repaired was not cheap and could not be carried out quickly, so we planned to damage the car and front room window.

At midnight, a couple of days later, we drove past the house and made sure that the lights were out and that no one was in the living-room. We pulled up round the corner and switched off the car lights and engine.

After a couple of minutes, just to make sure that all was quiet, I got out, carrying a brick in each hand, and walked around the corner and down to the house. The iron gate was closed. It had a little hoop of rope over the post. I quietly lifted the hoop and opened the gate, which gave a slight squeak as it opened. My heart was pounding, but I was determined to go through with the plan. As soon as I got to within about four feet of the window I raised my arm and threw one brick as hard as I could at the window. As I turned to run back to where Stan was waiting, I threw the second brick through the windscreen of Hugh's nice clean car, and although it failed to smash completely, it did shatter. The brick bounced off onto the bonnet, making a dent and scratching it.

By the time lights came on in the house and neighbouring houses, Stan had started the car and we were away.

'That was great,' I said 'We'll have to leave it for a while now, but I'm not going to let that man rest until he dies.'

'No problem, Rick,' said Stan. 'Anytime you want me, I'm there, mate.'

Over the next few days I searched the local papers for news of what had happened, but found nothing reported.

A few weeks later, when I was in the neighbourhood, I decided to drive past Hugh's house. I was not surprised to see that the front garden wall had been built higher, with a bigger garden gate. Two large gateposts and gates had been installed in front of the driveway, and in addition to the gates the car had a purpose-made cover over it.

I laughed. 'If he thinks that'll stop me, he'd better think again,' I said to myself.

It had been many years since I had found out about Mum's harrowing upbringing, and was curious to know whether Hugh had changed his phone number in that time. I still had the old one in my address book under 'N' for Nan, and although it had long since been scribbled over, I could still make it out. I was working away for a couple of weeks, and decided to make a call from a local phone booth close to the bed and breakfast where I was staying.

'Hello – is Hugh there, please?' I asked, as a woman who sounded very much like Avril answered the phone.

'Yes, he's in the garden,' she said. 'I'll call him. Who shall I say is calling?'

I had to think quickly.

'Oh, it's Bill from the garage; it's about his car.'

Avril went off, and I could hear her calling to him.

'Hugh! It's Bill from the garage on the phone for you… He's just coming, Bill,' she said briefly when she got back to the phone.

'Okay, thanks, ' I replied.

'Hello?' Hugh said in an unconcerned tone.

'Is that Hugh?' I said politely.

'Yes, this is Hugh here.'

I prepared myself for the next sentence.

'Well, Hugh, I am so glad you are in, as I will be round in about five minutes to break your fucking legs.'

I was surprised at the venomous voice that I just unleashed on Hugh.

'Who is this?' Hugh murmured, clearly shaken.

'It's your worst fucking nightmare come true, you fucking paedophile.'

The phone went dead. It was clear that Hugh had had the shock of his life. I put the phone down and found that I was shaking.

I had only intended to put the wind up Hugh, but to actually break his legs would have been a pleasure.

It was clear to me that the hatred that I had for Hugh had intensified as soon as I heard him speak. I knew that I had made a serious impact, and wondered what Hugh would be telling Avril now.

I was surprised at how much Hugh's voice had affected me. I knew at this point that if I bumped into Hugh in the street that I would have trouble in controlling my anger. I wondered whether I had given myself away by calling Hugh a paedophile, but then realized that Hugh could hardly tell anyone why a man would call him and threaten him and then call him a paedophile.

I walked back to the bed and breakfast and gradually calmed down. I called Stan and told him what I had done.

'Well done, mate,' said Stan. 'Let me have his number and I'll give him a call, too.'

I gave Stan the number and knew that if he ever rang Hugh, he'd frighten him as much as I had.

I slept well that night and woke up still thinking about the phone call, but I felt justified. I decided that the neighbours needed to know there was a paedophile living close to them, and who he was. I knew that some of them had been living within a couple of doors of Hugh and Avril for a long time, and wondered what they would have made of the fact that their daughter and their grandchildren had suddenly stopped coming to see them some years before. Armed with these thoughts I decided to write a short but concise letter for each of the twenty nearest neighbours spelling, out a few facts about their neighbour Hugh.

'Dear Homeowner,

I feel it my duty to inform you that Mr Harris who lives at No. 32 is a paedophile, and I would not want it on my conscience if anything happened to any members of your family. I know that he abused a girl from a very early age until she was sixteen, and that she continues to suffer from her experiences to this day. This is not a hoax or a malicious letter to bring shame on Mr Harris, but a warning to those living around him. I know he comes across as a decent man and that he has in the past invited his neighbours' children in to see his aviary birds. Please heed this warning and distance yourself from him. I aim to bring this man to justice and would ask that you treat this letter with confidence.'

A week later, my job had finished and I was ready to give out my letters. I was in two minds whether to post the letters or to deliver them by hand. I realized that they would have more impact if I delivered them myself. The following night, I walked up one side of the road and then down the other, posting the twenty letters that I had written but not signed. I had written the letters in stylized capitals. It did concern me that my handwriting could be traced but my instinct told me that all would be well.

As I drove away I noticed two of the householders were looking up and down the street from their windows. I could only presume that they had read the letters and were trying to see who had posted them.

As usual the only person I told what I had done was Stan, and as always, he gave me all the moral support I needed.

I decided to leave off from my planned vengeance for a while, but wanted to do one more thing for now. Hugh still kept a dog, but he had changed from keeping big Alsatians and now had a small terrier, which he walked in the same place that he had walked his other dogs for years. He would drive to the local country park and walk the dog for half an hour at five o'clock every day.

One day I pulled up at the park and waited for Hugh to arrive. Watching from a distance, I saw Hugh park and walk off into the country park with his dog.

I got out of my car, and, after looking around to check that the coast was clear, I opened the boot and took out a little spike that I used for carpentry work.

I walked over to Hugh's car and again checked that it was all clear before stooping down and stabbing each of the tyres. I knew that they would be flat by the time Hugh returned, and with only one spare tyre he would need to call a garage out to have his car transported away. In reality I would have preferred to follow Hugh into the country park and kill him, but I knew that I would eventually get caught if I took such drastic action. I wasn't a born killer, but if I thought that I could get away with it, then I would have killed him years before. I settled on the pleasure of tormenting.

I really did feel good after each of my acts. The adrenalin rush and the excitement were one thing, but the thought of Hugh not knowing who was doing it was even more satisfying.

At one point, I did consider that Hugh would narrow it down and assume that it was either Dad or I, but even if he did, it was highly unlikely that he would say anything. Hugh knew that he couldn't go to the police without risking exposure himself, so I was confident that I could go on tormenting Hugh for years.

PART FIVE:

LIFE AFTER MUM

19

HER STIFF AND LIFELESS BODY

I had always tried to buy the most up-to-date gadgets, and was actually known by my friends as 'Gadget Man'. I couldn't afford everything that I wanted, and was never that materialistic, but the gadgets I did buy were for the home and not necessarily for me.

I took Matthew shopping on a Saturday to have a look at a camcorder. A friend had recently bought one, and after watching the videos of my friend's children, I desperately wanted to capture my own children on film. Matthew was enjoying school and, like me, he loved sports such as gymnastics, football and trampolining. I desperately wanted to capture the highlights of his achievements, as I knew how special it would be to watch them in the years to come.

I looked at several camcorders. To my surprise, the shops were offering some good deals on buy now and pay in six months' time. I decided to fill the forms in and see whether I could obtain the credit required to take the camcorder home. As I had been in a mortgage agreement for nine years, the credit agreement was accepted with no questions asked.

I took Matthew and the new camcorder home. I couldn't wait to start filming Anne and children, and after I had read the instructions I managed to work it without too many problems. The children loved seeing themselves on TV, and were excited about being filmed with their Nan and Granddad on the following day when we were due to go for Sunday dinner.

I spent Sunday morning perfecting my skills on the new gadget and had the two sets of batteries charged. I had read the instructions in fine detail and had bought two additional video cartridges, as I wanted my first videos to be particularly good.

We arrived at Mum and Dad's house at around midday as planned, and it wasn't long before I was explaining to them how good the video recorder was.

It was 1991 and the mid-August sunshine was just perfect. Dad was chasing Matthew and Marie around the garden and lifting them up to pick the bright red apples off the neighbour's tree. The afternoon was turning out to be very memorable. Mum had prepared a cold meat salad to serve on the garden benches and tables that Dad had made. I was videoing the fun and laughter that we all shared together.

After eating our dinner we all went indoors to watch what I had videoed. Compact videos were fairly new then, and the children were really excited. I was good with the video and gave a running commentary on what was happening. The children had soon got used to being filmed, but it wasn't until they watched themselves on video that they realized how different they sounded.

That afternoon was one of the best times that we had had together as a family, and to see Mum smiling and full of happiness after all the difficulties of the past was very satisfying.

We said our goodbyes to Mum and Dad and made our way home. That evening we put the videos on again, and as we watched Dad, Mum and the children playing in the garden we were glad that we had managed to buy the video camera despite the difficult financial circumstances.

Times were difficult in the building industry, but Dad and I had managed to find regular work in London for a couple of property developers who needed maintenance work carried out on their properties. We didn't much like commuting to London everyday, as the drive could take up to two hours each way. The mortgage rates were very high, and the cost of living was stretching everybody to the limit, but we were just about managing to keep our bills paid.

We were both very versatile and could undertake most types of building work, which helped us to win small contracts that kept us busy for about three weeks of the month.

The following morning, Dad picked me up to travel to London for our day's work. I took the camcorder with me, and as we travelled through the East End of London I videoed the areas where Dad had grown up before he was evacuated in 1941.

We were now enjoying working together more than ever, and we talked about how good Sunday afternoon had been. I told Dad about how I had had problems getting the kids to bed, as they wanted to watch the video of the afternoon over and over.

Dad told me that, unusually, Mum had slept through the night, and that he had left her in bed rather than disturb her. It was unusual for Mum not to be up before Dad, as she would normally be downstairs making his tea and preparing his sandwiches for the day. They slept in separate bedrooms now, as Dad was prone to snore, but never a day went by that he would be up before Mum. On this occasion Dad was happy that she had slept through the night, and just put it down to the energetic Sunday fun and games with the grandchildren. He hoped that this was the start of her sleeping a lot better.

That evening, Dad dropped me off and drove the remaining five miles back home, looking forward to his evening meal with Mum. When he opened the front door he was shocked to see the hallway had been strewn with paper, and there were some settee pillows on the floor.

Dad could sense instantly that something was wrong.

'Rose!' he shouted. 'Where are you?'

When he got no reply, he ran upstairs, and as he entered her bedroom he could see that Mum was still in bed.

Mum had two dogs, a mongrel puppy and the Jack Russell that she had had for about seven years. Dad had seen the puppy downstairs, lying on the settee, but the Jack Russell was lying on the bed, curled up behind Mum's back on top of the covers.

Dad was confused. He struggled to compute why she was still in bed. She would normally have had dinner on and welcomed him through the door. He leant over Mum. She looked as though she were asleep. He knew she had some tablets in the house that would help her to sleep if she needed them. He felt her hand, which was cold and clammy. So did her head.

He had no experience in first aid except what he had learnt in the army, but that was too long ago to be of any use now. He decided to call the doctor, then call me.

'Rick, get down here now; I can't wake Mum. Her back is warm, but I just can't wake her.'

I knew that something was drastically wrong. I had a motorbike, and in just a few minutes I pulled up outside the house having run every red light on the way. When I went into the bedroom, I felt Mum's brow and hands. She was very cold to the touch.

'Have you phoned anyone, Dad?' I asked.

'I've called the doctor,' said Dad.

'I'm calling an ambulance, Dad. You stay with Mum.'

I ran down the stairs and picked up the phone in the hallway.

'Hello? Can I have an ambulance, please?' I said as the emergency operator answered.

'What is the problem?' she asked, after taking my name and Dad's address.

'It's my mum; we can't wake her. Her head and hands are cold and clammy, but her body's warm.'

'Is she breathing?' asked the operator.

'I don't know,' I said.

'Listen to her mouth, and if possible see if you can find a pulse.'

I had to shout instructions up to Dad.

'Dad! Is Mum breathing? Listen to her mouth.'

After a few seconds Dad shouted back, 'I can't tell, Rick.'

I relayed the information back to the operator who told me that Dad should get Mum on to the floor.

'Dad! Get Mum on the floor, onto a hard surface.'

A few seconds later, I heard a thump on the floor, followed by a harrowing cry from Dad and immediately dropped the phone.

'Get up here now, Rick!'

When I entered the bedroom I could see Dad standing by Mum's body on the floor. Mum's body had gone into rigor mortis, and in the narrow space between the bed and the wall her body was still curled up just as it had been when she fell asleep.

Dad and me stared at each other in disbelief. After a few silent seconds, we lifted her stiff and lifeless body back onto the bed and covered it with the duvet.

Both of us were in a total state of shock.

Dad wandered off downstairs in a zombie-like state, and I decided to lie on the bed next to Mum. She looked as if she were just sleeping, and it wasn't until the sirens from the ambulance brought me out of my reverie that it started to dawn on me that Mum had died just five days before her fiftieth birthday.

I immediately telephoned Victoria. She arrived within five minutes and began to try to comfort Dad. He was still in a state of severe shock, sitting in a chair staring into space with tears streaming down his face. Victoria tried to talk to him, but he could not even acknowledge what was going on around him.

When the ambulance crew arrived they immediately went into the bedroom, and quickly confirmed that there was nothing they could do for Mum. They explained that they had telephoned a doctor to pronounce that Mum had died, and that they would have to wait for a different vehicle to take her body away.

We had been planning a surprise birthday for Mum's fiftieth, and everything was ready. Sixty people had been invited to the party, and John was going to play live music with the reggae band that he had recently joined. John had worked for me for a short while about six years before, and when I had struggled to pay him for some work he had done I offered him a saxophone in part payment, which I had bought for myself but had not been able to master.

John accepted the saxophone, and within three months he had mastered the saxophone to a level where he was accepted in a fledgling reggae band.

Mum had known all the band members. They would often turn up at the house on a weekend with John and just jam in the garden. Mum loved it; she used to look forward to the times when some of the band members would bring their children round.

Family and friends had been informed about the party and been told to keep it quiet from Mum. I knew that it would be my responsibility to telephone everyone and give them the tragic news.

The first person that I contacted was Elizabeth.

'Hello Elizabeth, it's Rick,' I said in a sombre voice.

'Hi, Rick, how are you?' she replied in her usual happy voice, before I could get any more words out.

'Elizabeth, I have some bad news.'

She could hear from my voice that I wasn't messing around. She was used to having a laugh with me on the phone, but she knew instantly that this was different.

'Mum's dead,' I said in a low voice.

'What do you mean – Mum's dead?'

I was struggling to get the words out but finally I managed to tell her.

'Dad got home from work today and Mum had died in her sleep.'

All I could hear was a scream at the other end of the phone.

'Elizabeth! Elizabeth! Are you there?'

'Hello – what's happened?' said a new voice.

'Who's that?' I said.

'It's Carol – I'm Elizabeth's neighbour. I was in the garden and heard her scream, so I came in the back door and found her on the floor.'

I explained what had happened, and asked Carol to stay with her until I could arrange someone to collect her.

I then phoned John and David. Fortunately they were both at home, and after they collected Elizabeth they arrived at the house within half an hour.

Over the next couple of hours, some of Dad's family members arrived to offer their support. I spent the evening telephoning everyone who knew Mum and Dad.

The reaction of most of them was one of shock, and some wouldn't take me seriously at first. This was hardly surprising, because I had a good sense of humour normally and I was well-known for my practical jokes.

Then I telephoned Nan to give her the awful news. I had put off calling her until all of the family who lived nearby had been informed. It had been only eleven years since Mum and Nan had been reunited, and it felt so unfair. The call didn't last long, but I promised that I would call the following day when Nan had had time to absorb what had happened.

Elizabeth decided to stay with Dad for the night until we could work out what needed to be done next. She and Dad had had their moments, and there had been some animosity between them in the past, but all that was forgotten now. Elizabeth knew that, despite her own anguish, Dad would need her now.

Over the next week or so, Dad's brothers and sisters offered their full support and helped us arrange Mum's funeral. I kept myself busy. Subconsciously I had not fully absorbed the gravity of what had happened, and it was not until a day or two before the funeral that I started to become deeply affected by Mum's passing. I couldn't help thinking that the medication she was on was partly responsible for her death, though I had no way to prove it and for now there was too much to do rather than look for someone to blame.

The autopsy indicated that cholesterol was a significant factor and that Mum's blood pressure was very low, but I *was* sure that Hugh played a significant part in her death: although it wasn't apparent to anyone, it was clear to me. I knew I needed to pay Hugh a visit, but it would have to be when I was thinking properly. I knew that if I approached Hugh now, it would probably result in me being locked up.

*

Mum had always made it clear that she wanted to be cremated; she had a fear of spiders, and although we never had any serious conversations about death and our preferences, she always said, 'I definitely do not want to end up six feet down in a wooden box.' Dad on the other hand preferred the burial option, but they never really made any firm decisions – and why should they? There were no signs that either of them would be dying anytime soon.

Ten days after Mum's death, her coffin was brought back to the house so she could spend one last evening there before the cremation.

Some of the family and friends arrived in the evening to pay their last respects. The funeral directors had dressed her in one of her favourite dresses, and had prepared her hair and makeup just as she would have done it herself for an evening out with Dad. I visited the house that evening, and spent some time holding Mum's hand and reminiscing. She lay motionless but looked very much alive.

Before I left her, I noticed that a Red Admiral butterfly had settled on the ceiling directly above Mum's coffin, but didn't give it too much thought, and after ensuring that Dad was okay, I said good night and went home to Anne and the kids in a very sombre mood.

I had trouble sleeping that night, and wasn't looking forward to the day ahead. When I got to the house, the delivery vans were arriving every ten minutes or so, and within a short time the front garden was covered in flowers of all shapes and sizes. The coffin lid was still off and those who wanted to, were invited to say their last goodbyes and to put messages in the coffin. Dad sat in the room with the coffin as he had done all night.

It was sad to see how the loss of Mum had affected him. He had changed so much since the day Mum died that we were starting to worry about how he would cope in the long term. I knew more than anyone what a deep thinker Dad was, and what he was capable of.

I placed a photo of Anne, the children and me in the coffin. Before leaving the room, I noticed that the Red Admiral butterfly was still on the ceiling above the coffin. Some years before, I had bought Mum a glass dome that had flowers and two stuffed butterflies inside it. Mum always expressed her love for them, so I thought it was fitting that the Red Admiral was still there.

The funeral directors eventually arrived and fixed the lid on the coffin. I was in the room when they screwed the lid down and it was at this point that I broke down. I had been so busy making arrangements and keeping my mind occupied on other things, I don't think that I had allowed myself to really believe Mum was gone.

Elizabeth comforted me, although she was struggling with her own emotions, and I was so glad to have her close by.

There was a huge gathering of our family members, neighbours and friends outside the house, and it was a sad sight to see the coffin being placed in the hearse before the slow drive to the crematorium.

Even at the crematorium, the turnout was huge. All Dad's family and friends were there, along with Nan and her family. Mum had been very popular, and had no enemies whatsoever. It was her young age that surprised everyone; forty-nine was not old, and Mum was the first of the large family to die since my father's mother some twelve years before.

20

DAD'S DECLINE

At the time of Mum's death and even after her funeral, Dad seemed to be in a trance. Although his suffering was to be expected, no one knew how much he was truly hurting. He had always kept his feelings locked up, and even now found it hard to show his emotions. Later on, I discovered that he had cried himself to sleep every night since Mum died.

Elizabeth and myself had arranged the wake for Mum back at the house that she had lived in for the past twenty-two years. Dad was happy for us to arrange for John's band to attend to play some of the reggae music as he knew how much Mum had loved to listen to the band.

When everyone had arrived there were hushed voices and discussions going on in various parts of the house about how much Mum was going to be missed and how she had left her mark on everybody she came in contact with. Some of the older family members were preparing sandwiches and pouring drinks while others were chatting in the garden.

Dad sat in the living room below a large framed picture of Mum that he had ordered from the local photography studio. As the day wore on and melted into the evening, a party atmosphere was starting to develop in the garden. Afterwards, it came to light that some of the neighbours, who didn't really know Mum well, thought this was inappropriate. We didn't care about what they said as we knew that Mum would have wanted everyone to celebrate her life rather than sit around and mope.

Dad chose not to drink too much and satisfied himself with cups of tea and the odd glass of Southern Comfort. He knew that if he indulged in too much alcohol there would be a strong possibility that he would get emotional, which he wanted to avoid. His older sisters and some other family members and close friends sat in the living room with him, but found it difficult to know what to talk about for the six or seven hours they spent there.

Dad stayed strong during the day and the evening, and was happy with the support that he had. When the older family members left, there were still many of us in the garden, including our cousins and many other friends of our family. John's band members were in the garden entertaining everyone with quiet sentimental songs.

John played some solo saxophone, which mesmerized everyone, and I was busy capturing the evening on my video camera. John was on top form, and it was heart-rending to hear him play for Mum while everyone sat around in admiration. To hear the band quietly sing Mum's favourites such as Bob Marley's *No Woman, No Cry* and *One Love*, brought tears to everybody's eyes. But they were not necessarily just tears of unhappiness: we were celebrating Mum's life, and with the beautiful music and mixed emotions of the day, it was not surprising that everyone was touched.

Nan and her family listened with tears in their eyes; they only wished that they had had the privilege of knowing Mum for longer than they had. Nan in particular was clearly struggling to cope with Mum's death and although I could see that she was holding herself together in front of many people that she didn't know, I also knew that it would be a long time before she got over it.

As everybody left to go at about 2:00am, we all said our goodbyes to Dad, who was still sitting in the living room with Aunty Victoria and Uncle William. Elizabeth had decided to stay with Dad since Mum's death, but she knew that she would have to get back to her normal routine soon. Elizabeth, John and David and myself got together the following day to discuss how we would ensure that Dad was not left alone for too long. We knew that he would find it difficult to cope without Mum.

Despite the difficult times that Mum and Dad had been through personally, it was obvious that they loved each other unconditionally, and to think of Dad being on his own worried us. The August weather had been very hot, and it was agreed that we would each take turns in visiting Dad regularly during the next few weeks and invite him round for dinner and weekend barbecues. I was particularly worried about Dad, as he had said something to me for no apparent reason about one year before. We were driving to a job and just chatting generally, when Dad said out of the blue, 'If anything ever happens to Mum I'm going to join her.'

'What do you mean by that, Dad?' I had said inquisitively. 'Mum's not ill; don't say things like that, Dad.'

'Well I'm just telling you that if she dies before me,' Dad replied, 'I will follow her, whether its tomorrow or in thirty years' time.'

I changed the subject and never mentioned it to anyone, but I knew that he was a man who meant what he said. I decided to put the thought behind me, but now that Mum had died, it was on my mind.

As the next few weeks and months passed by, Dad seemed to be coping reasonably well, but as Christmas approached, we knew that it was going to be difficult for all of us, in particular for Dad. We arranged to get together regularly, ensuring that Dad didn't have much time alone. He enjoyed playing with his four grandchildren and making them laugh, and it was a pleasure for us to see him so happy.

He seemed to be improving, and by Spring Dad was able to come back to work with me for a brief period. Although I think he was glad of the structure of the working day, after several months, he seemed to be getting worse and work was becoming too much for him.

Dad found it difficult to go home to an empty house every night. He didn't like to be a burden, and although we wanted him to visit us more he became very withdrawn. He told us that he couldn't bear to be in the house any longer, and that he was starting to have nightmares about when he had found Mum's lifeless body in her bed. Unable to take it any longer, he had decided to sell the house and buy a Dutch tug to live on, and take it across to France to tour the canals and waterways. This was the first positive step he had taken in a long time, and the whole family supported his action.

'I can't wait to get the tug,' he told me. 'I just need to get away and concentrate on new things.'

Dad was a man who needed to be doing things, and who was not comfortable visiting people even though he hated being alone. Until Mum died he had never been alone, and he was struggling to cope with this new way of life. He knew that being on the boat would be difficult, but he had weighed up the pros and cons and figured that the new environment and constant need for planning would help him to avoid the melancholy thoughts that he feared.

As he and Mum had been council tenants for over thirty years, they had been offered the house at a hugely reduced rate, as the government of the day was promoting home ownership and selling off a percentage of older council houses. While the house was on the market, Dad planned his immediate future, and visited many marinas and boat yards to look at the boats that he had found for sale in various magazines.

He eventually travelled to Belgium in April 1992 to look at a 50-foot Dutch canal tug. He knew it would need some modifications but decided that it was exactly what he was looking for.

The tug needed some renovation work, but it was mostly cosmetic, and to Dad it was a project that he could manage while he travelled. Having secured a loan from the bank as a deposit for the boat against the forthcoming sale of the house, he was excited about the future, and spent many hours gathering all the information he would need for his new life: from English Channel navigational charts to French canal charts, he left nothing to chance. He had even bought French phrase books and was learning the basics as he knew it would be important, specifically for navigation and VHF radio contact with ports and marinas.

As June approached Dad became more excited, and we were pleased to see that he had something that really took his mind off of the negative thoughts that had been dominating him over the winter period. He spent much of June planning the final navigational details for his epic trip and maintaining contact with the boat brokerage company, trying to finalise a delivery date for the tug.

By June Dad had sold the house and was staying with a friend while waiting for the tug to be delivered to a marina on the south coast. Despite his excitement and although we knew what he was planning, he kept much of the details to himself and just told us that everything was going to plan. However, by this stage Dad and I were not only father and son, we were like best friends, and I was slightly concerned that Dad had not discussed any of his plans in detail. I decided to try and find out what the situation was.

'What's the latest news on the tug these days?' I asked one day when Dad came for Sunday dinner.

'Oh, everything's going to plan,' he told me. 'The tug arrives next week, so I will be going to the marina to live on it until I've prepared everything for the trip to France.'

'Oh, that's great, Dad! Let me know when it arrives. I'd love to come and see it.' I wanted Dad to know how excited I was too, and that I was only too willing to help him ready the tug for the voyage.

The end of June came and went, as did July and August. Dad explained that there had been a problem with the tug as it was being brought over from Belgium. He had been told that the engine had overheated and that the tug had had to return to port for the engine to be fixed.

It had been over a year now since Mum had died. Dad and I spent many hours visiting marinas, looking at boats and just walking along sea walls, enjoying the views. When we were younger, I had helped Dad build a speedboat from scratch, which we had great adventures on. Dad was always tinkering and enjoyed the challenge of renovating boats and putting his own stamp on them. His love of the sea was contagious and we were both men of the sea in our hearts. Between us we had enjoyed many weekends windsurfing, water-skiing, sailing or just mucking around on the beach with family and friends.

At the same time, work was difficult to find, and I was struggling to meet my financial commitments. I knew it wasn't the answer, but these worries seemed to fade away as quickly as they had come upon me when I drank. My problems and my drinking grew in tandem; somehow I could always find enough money to go to the pub, despite Anne's protests.

Interest rates were high, and as I was the sole breadwinner, I found it difficult to make ends meet. I knew that Dad couldn't work, not through the want of trying but because his mind was on his new life on the tug.

I was the sort of person who would grab the bull by the horns and get on and do things rather than talk about it. I discussed the options with Anne, and it was clear that something drastic would have to be done if we did not want to lose the house.

I spoke to some friends, and as I was not prepared to work for less than it cost me to live, I took up an offer to go to Abu Dhabi and stay with a friend of a friend – Bob – to look for work for two weeks. I had been told that there was plenty of construction work, and as I had managed building sites I thought I would have a good chance of finding work within that time.

I made arrangements with my friend and in early October 1992 I was on my way to Abu Dhabi.

By the time we arrived it was late, even so the heat as I stepped off the plane was suffocating. Once inside the terminal, I was overwhelmed by the opulent design and colours. Inside the terminal there was a vast, ornate dome, psychedelic and alien, shaped almost like the cap of a huge concrete mushroom. Blearily, I walked underneath its canopy, struggling to process what I was looking at – I had never seen anything like it in my life, and it quickly dawned on me how different life in the Middle East was going to be.

I was collected by Bob who was waiting in the arrivals area for me with a piece of paper in his hand with my name on it.

'Hi, Rick,' Bob said as we met.

'Hi, Bob, great to meet you. 'I was feeling nervous and wondered whether I had made the right decision.

As we left the airport, I was surprised by the humidity and warmth of the evening. It was 11:00pm before we arrived at Bob's apartment. It was directly over an Indian takeaway, which we decided to visit.

The following morning Bob gave me some addresses to visit and submit my CV. My friend Joe had helped me arrange the trip and he had also helped me to compile a CV with Bob's landline as my contact number. Joe had asked Bob to source the local agencies so that I could approach them on my arrival.

I wasted no time, and the following morning I was off to the employment agencies. I had been told that sending my CV from the UK was a waste of time, because the local agencies weren't prepared to put a candidate forward unless they had interviewed them personally. On the first day, I delivered my CV to three agencies, who showed an interest and told me that they had clients who they would forward it on to. Although I was excited and felt confident about the prospect, I didn't have any experience of working abroad and I thought that would work against me.

I had thought that the United Arab Emirates was a dry state, and had not expected to get a beer, but that evening Bob took me out to the local hotel, where to my surprise we could get a drink in the bar. I was secretly very happy as I missed the feeling that alcohol gave me.

Bob was a lecturer at the local military base and didn't like to stay out too late, so we went back to the apartment and played darts before going to bed at 11:00pm.

The following day I set out again to visit some building companies that Bob had identified and again I passed on my CV. Then I headed back to Bob's apartment for the afternoon, as most sites closed down from midday until 3:00pm, due to the sweltering heat.

When the phone rang, I answered it, expecting to hear someone asking to speak to Bob, but to my surprise it was one of the agencies. They wanted me to come and see them urgently, as they had two clients who were interested in meeting me that day. I couldn't believe it, and the excitement filled my whole body. The opportunities back home were few and far between, so it was a real shock to get this much interest so quickly.

I went to the agency and they gave me the names and addresses of the clients that I had to meet later that afternoon. Taxis were very cheap, and as Abu Dhabi was a relatively small place I decided to make use of them. The first interview was for a position as a finishing foreman on a high-class hotel project, and they made an offer to me there and then on a wage that I would have accepted, but I knew I would have to attend the second interview before making a decision. I told the company that I would contact them in the morning when I had made a decision.

I attended the second interview, and again was offered a six-month contract there and then, subject to a three-month probationary period. This time the position was as a site manager on projects for a sheikh. The package was better than the previous offer and it sounded much more exciting, so I accepted the offer. It was agreed that I would start in two weeks' time, after the necessary paperwork had been prepared.

I telephoned Anne that evening to tell her and the children the news, but when she answered, the full realisation hit me and I broke down in floods of tears. I hadn't expected to be offered a job so quickly, and the prospect of being able to clear my mounting debts back home and work as a professional site manager did excite me, but I had mixed emotions. I loved Anne and our children immensely, and the thought of not seeing them for six months hadn't crossed my mind seriously before.

After pulling myself together I started to explain to Anne what had occurred.

'Anne, I've been offered two jobs in the same day, and I've accepted one of them.'

'Oh, my god! That's great,' replied Anne. 'When do you start?'

'Well, I'm coming home as planned next week, and then the company are going to provide me with a ticket to return once they have prepared the work visa and accommodation.'

We chatted for a short while, and I spoke to Matthew and Marie. That was very difficult, because I knew I was going to find being away from them very tough, but ultimately they were the reason why I had taken the job.

I enjoyed the remainder of my time in Abu Dhabi, and spent time swimming and snorkelling in the clear waters of the Arabian Gulf. I returned home as planned, and after four days with my family, I was back on a plane to Abu Dhabi to start my new career. The company had arranged for me to stay in one of the main hotels in Abu Dhabi, which was owned by the sheikh I was working for. I was given a company car and, within a few days, I started to plan the work on one of the palaces owned by the sheikh.

I telephoned Anne and the kids as often as I could and I loved to hear their news. Even though we both knew that working abroad was the best thing I could do for the family, it was very tough on Anne. I had left her with two young children who would often play up because their Dad wasn't there, so I made a point of checking in with her every chance I got. I wanted to stay in touch with day-to-day household life.

I also made a point of calling my sister, who was keeping an eye on Dad. He had moved into a static caravan while waiting for the tug, but Elizabeth was alarmed by his increasingly depressed, lethargic state and insisted he stay with her.

Elizabeth told me that she had received a call from the hospital to explain that they had put Dad on anti-depressants after he admitted that he was considering taking his own life. The news shocked us both to the core. We knew Dad was feeling low, but for him to consider taking his own life frightened us and we were desperately worried about him. A chill ran through my body as I recalled what Dad had said in the car about joining Mum. I knew Dad didn't say things like that light-heartedly, and I didn't quite know what I could do.

I tried to calm her down and we went through what she would say to Dad when he came home. Dad finally returned at teatime and when Elizabeth confronted him, he broke down and sobbed in Elizabeth's arms.

'I can't go on like this – I miss Mum so much, and everything is going wrong.'

Elizabeth was crying too, but she tried to reassure Dad that everything would be okay soon. She knew he missed me, and that the tug having not arrived was a big issue, but she didn't want to make him more upset by questioning him about it.

'Dad,' she said, 'I'm going to arrange for John and David to come round for Christmas dinner so we can all enjoy it, and if you're up for it, you're welcome to stay here until then – until the tug is ready, in fact.'

'I don't know if I can hold out love,' sobbed Dad. 'I want to be with Mum.'

Elizabeth didn't know what to do or say, but she knew he was close to the edge and that she had to let John and David know.

*

I couldn't take my mind off of the situation back home. I knew Dad was hurting bad, and I wanted to be there for him. After a sleepless night, I called Elizabeth.

'Hi, how are things?' I said when she picked up the phone.

Elizabeth had been expecting my call and took it upstairs.

'Dad's downstairs at the moment,' she told me, 'and he's feeling slightly better today. He has good and bad days at the moment. I told him you would be ringing, and he is looking forward to speaking to you.'

'Okay, can you put him on, and then I'll speak to you before I go.'

'Will do, Rick. Hang on there...I'll get Dad to pick the phone up downstairs, hang on a minute...'

'Hello Rick, are you there?'

'Dad, it's great to hear your voice. How are you?'

'Oh, not too bad, son. I'm struggling without Mum, though. I can't stop thinking about her, and what with Christmas coming, it's getting to me, to be honest.' Dad's voice was very subdued, and he was having difficulty getting his words out.

'Yes, so I hear, Dad. Look – you have Elizabeth, John and David there, so make sure you go and see them if you're feeling low. They'll support you and make sure that you get the help you need, if that's what it takes.' I was feeling really guilty that I couldn't be there with Dad, and it made me feel sick to the stomach to hear him so despondent and yet be unable to hug him or look him in the eye.

'Please promise me that you won't talk about killing yourself, Dad. I know it's hard, but after Christmas things will be better; and you can come out and spend some time with me if you like.'

'I'm sorry, Rick. I didn't mean to upset anyone, but I was having a particularly bad day, and hoped that I could get some medication to take the thoughts away. I'm okay now, and as you say, things will get better.'

'That's the way, Dad. You always said to me that it's a joy to be alive; so remember that, and you know Mum wouldn't want you being down.'

I didn't know what else to say, but I felt sure that Dad was just reaching out for help. I reasoned with myself that Dad couldn't really be suicidal with such a large supportive family who loved him so much.

We said our goodbyes, and Dad passed the phone back to Elizabeth, who was now downstairs.

'I feel much better, having spoken to Dad,' I said. 'He sounds like he is going to fight his demons – and, knowing Dad, he will beat them.' I was trying to sound positive, but in reality I was desperately worried. 'Keep me informed of things, please, Elizabeth. You can always leave a message at the hotel if you want me to contact you.'

'Okay Rick, well, you take care of yourself, and we'll speak again soon.'

Elizabeth hung up and sat down with Dad, who was sitting with his head in his hands.

'Are you alright Dad?'

'Yes, I'm okay love. I'm just sorry that I've caused you all so much worry.'

'Don't be so daft, Dad,' said Elizabeth, putting her arms around him. 'We're all here for you, that's what families are for, isn't it?'

Dad took a deep breath and sat up.

'You're right, love. I'll be fine, you'll see.'

21

EMERGENCY

I continued with my work in Abu Dhabi and phoned home every other day to find out how Dad was. I was pleased to hear that he was spending time visiting family and friends. I knew that Dad was at his most vulnerable if he had nothing to take his mind off of the past. Then, on the seventeenth of December when I phoned home, I was given the news that I had dreaded.

'Rick, your Dad has been to the hospital again, and he's told the doctor that unless he gives him a bed and sedates him, he is going to kill himself.' Anne's voice was trembling as she told me what Elizabeth had told her earlier that day.

'That's it, I'm coming home,' I told her. 'Get a message to Elizabeth and tell her I'll be home in the next day or two.'

The next morning I went to the head office to see my manager.

'Tony, I have a family emergency at home that I must return to the UK to deal with for a week or two.'

Tony was my immediate boss, and knew that my dad was struggling to deal with the loss of Mum.

'It's not really up to me to agree, Rick,' he said, 'but I'll speak to the sheikh's adviser, Mohammed, and see what we can do.'

'Thanks, Tony,' I said with sincerity. 'I'll pay for my own flight, and I don't expect to be paid while I am off, but it is important that I go, as my dad really needs my support.'

Tony was a good man and said he would do what he could. He liked me, and despite Mohammed's assumption that I was pretending to have problems so that I could spend time my family at Christmas, Tony convinced him otherwise.

Later that day, Tony arrived at the site that I was running to give me the good news.

'Mohammed has agreed that you can go; but he's not happy so, when you do return, keep your head down and don't go having time off.'

'Thanks Tony, I won't let you down.' I was really relieved and told Tony that I needed to go and arrange a flight. 'No need, Rick. I asked the secretary to do it. You're leaving in ten hours' time, and I've paid for it. We'll sort out the money when you return.'

Tony had no intention of taking the money from me. He had ways and means to cover the cost, and knew that I was still trying to pay off my debts back home. He had lost his own father the year before while he was working in the Middle East, so he had real empathy with my plight.

I couldn't wait to tell Anne that I would be home the following day, and was excited about being able to spend Christmas with the kids.

'Hello Anne,' I said as she answered the phone. 'I have some great news: I'll be on a plane in a few hours and home for two weeks.'

'Oh Rick, that's great news.'

Anne made arrangements for David to collect me at the airport, and she telephoned the family to tell them the good news. She arranged for my brothers and sister and her children to come round for dinner on the following Sunday. Although it had only been two months since I went to Abu Dhabi, it seemed much longer. I had worked away on the odd occasion when I had my own business, but it was only for a few days at a time, and I knew the kids were eager to hear about my exploits abroad.

As soon as I had arrived at the airport and collected my luggage, I rushed toward the arrivals gate expecting to see my brother David. When I saw the children and Anne there too, I couldn't stop myself from becoming emotional, I was so happy to see them. It was ten in the evening, so I really hadn't expected them to be there. Matthew and Marie were so happy to see me. I was the one who would always make them laugh; I would even encourage them to be slightly mischievous, but without being naughty, and they had missed that a lot, even if they had not realized it.

'Hello darling,' I said as I picked Marie up. I loved the children equally, but although Matthew was my little soldier, Marie was my little doll. Bystanders would have thought that I had been away for years, by the way we were all cuddling and crying. Having a close relationship with my kids meant so much to me. I had really missed having Matthew around me, he used to go everywhere with me and it would be a joy to have him follow me around again.

We made our way to David's car and set off on the two-hour ride home. After about thirty minutes, when I had told the children a few of my experiences in the desert, and about the camels that seemed to just roam around, the children gradually dropped off to sleep.

'That's good, isn't it?' I said. 'I'm telling them my stories and they fall asleep!' I knew the children would have been very tired, and I always tried to make light of situations.

'So how's Dad at the moment, Dave?' I asked once the children were fast asleep.

'Oh, he's not too bad Rick, but he is up and down emotionally.'

'Has he said any more about taking his own life again?' I had wanted to ask that question since I landed, but knew the time had to be right.

'No, he's been staying with Elizabeth, the hospital refused to give him a bed and sent him away with more tablets. Elizabeth has been trying to keep him preoccupied with things, and so far he hasn't mentioned it again. She's told him you will be home tomorrow, and he said he's looking forward to seeing you.'

I welled up. It was as much as I could do to stop myself from bursting into tears. I felt guilty about going abroad, and could not help thinking that Dad wouldn't have been so depressed had I not gone. David and Anne could sense my difficulty in keeping my emotions suppressed, but it was something we had all had to do.

We arrived home very late, and David and I carried the children to their bedrooms.

'Thanks for picking me up, Dave,' I said, 'We'll see you in the next day or two.'

'Okay Rick, let me know when you're meeting up with Dad, and if he's up for it, perhaps we will all go for a beer.' We said our goodbyes and David drove off, leaving Anne and I at the door waving him off.

'I'm so glad you managed to come home for Christmas, Rick,' said Anne. 'It just wouldn't have been the same without you.'

'I'm glad too, Anne, but let's not forget why I came home. I haven't really earned enough to take a holiday – this is about my dad.'

I didn't want to sound harsh or uncaring, but I had had plenty of time to think on the long flight home, and had it not been for the severity of the situation I would still have been in Abu Dhabi.

The following day, I was up early and on the phone to Elizabeth.

'Hi, Rick, it's great to hear your voice again. How was the flight home?'

After a brief chat I got down to the reason why I was phoning.

'Is Dad there?' I asked. I couldn't wait to speak to Dad, I had missed him more than I had imagined.

'I'll go and get him Rick. He's checking my car out for me, I think it needs some oil'

I could hear Elizabeth calling out to Dad.

'Dad! Rick's on the phone…He's just coming, Rick. We're looking forward to seeing you, and hearing all about Abu Dhabi.'

'Hello Rick,' said Dad, picking up the phone.

I had a lump in my throat and was so happy to hear his voice.

'Hello Dad, are you a mechanic now?' I was trying to break the ice and act normally, but inside I wasn't feeling normal at all.

The conversation could easily have been between a father and son who had no worries in the world between them, but that was so far from the truth.

We arranged to meet up at my house in a couple of days, when all the family would be there for dinner. In the meantime me, Elizabeth and my brothers had worked out how we would keep Dad preoccupied by going with him to visit his brothers and sisters and other family members. We knew that as Christmas approached he could become depressed very quickly if he was left alone for any length of time.

As arranged, Anne prepared a meal for us all one Sunday a few days before Christmas, and it was agreed that Dad would stay with us until Christmas day, when we would all meet at David's for Christmas dinner.

Dad and I spent the next few days going to marinas and looking at boats. We even went to the marina where the tug now lay, having been brought over from Belgium at last. We didn't go on the tug, but just looked at it from a distance. I was confused, but assumed that Dad had his reasons for not wanting to start work on renovating the tug. I thought it could have been the cold weather, or that Dad wanted to get Christmas out of the way before starting on his project and his new life. All he said was that he wasn't ready to take it just yet.

Christmas came and went, and although the children enjoyed themselves it was apparent to all of us that Christmases were no longer going to be the happy periods that we had all enjoyed in previous years.

Just after Christmas, Dad went to stay with John, who called me early one morning.

'Rick, the truck's been stolen. Dad was about to go to David's this morning, but when we went outside, it wasn't there. He's in a terrible state. You know how he feels about that truck. He loved taking Mum on caravanning trips with it.'

'What do you mean, it's been stolen?' My heart skipped a beat; I knew I was going to have to do something, and quickly.

'Rick, Dad is beside himself. He's crying and I'm not sure what to do.'

'Stay there, John, and don't let Dad out of your sight. I'll be there in ten minutes. You call the police and tell them what's happened.'

I was up and out of the door like a shot, and arrived at John's within ten minutes. Dad had managed to collect himself by the time I arrived, and John had agreed with the police that Dad would be accompanied to the station to report the theft, as the police station was very close to where John lived.

After Dad had given the police the details of the truck and filled out the paperwork, the police looked through their records of the previous night and told him that his truck had not actually been stolen.

'Your vehicle has not been stolen sir, it was involved in an accident with a stolen car last night, and had to be transported to a compound as it was in a dangerous position.'

We all felt immediately relieved. I drove Dad to the compound to look at the truck. We found out that a stolen car had ploughed into it at such a speed that it had forced the truck away from its parking spot and into the middle of the road. It was so badly damaged that it could not be pushed out of the way and so had to be transported by pickup.

The truck was a rear-engined design, and as the stolen car had hit it full on in the rear, it was clear that it was going to be a right-off. Dad only had third-party insurance, and even before he contacted his insurance company he knew it was futile to even think that they would cover the cost.

When Mum had died sixteen months earlier, Dad had given her car to John as he didn't have one at the time. John knew what he had to do, and immediately offered it back to Dad. Dad had never been without a vehicle, and took up John's offer, telling him however that he would let him have the car back as soon as he had moved onto the tug.

PART SIX:

FALLING INTO AN ABYSS

22

MORE GOODBYES

We spent New Year at David's house and although Dad put on a brave face, it was clear that he was not himself. It was difficult for us all to celebrate when the clock struck twelve, but we raised a glass to Mum, the mother, wife and grandmother who was missed beyond belief by all of us, but in particular by Dad. Previous New Year's Eves would have gone on until the early hours of the morning, but this one was over and done with by 1:00am.

I was due to return to Abu Dhabi on the third of January, which was Marie's eighth birthday. I knew it would be difficult for us all and especially for me and Marie, to say goodbye on her birthday was heart-wrenching. I desperately wanted to be there for her day, but I could do nothing about it. Their future was in my hands.

I spent the next two days with Dad and the rest of the family, discussing the future and how Dad was looking forward to getting the tug. I was still confused as to why Dad had not taken delivery of the tug, but decided to keep my thoughts to myself.

I had arranged for my cousin Kevin to take me to the airport at 5:00am and Dad had agreed to come along. Anne, Dad and myself got up at 4:00am. We had agreed to wake the kids at 4:30am so that I could spend a little time with them before I left. I didn't know how long it would be before I would see them again – it could be up to six months

'Wake up, kids. I'm going soon. Happy birthday, darling,' I said to Marie as she opened her eyes. 'Here's a little present for you now, but Mum has your other presents, which you can have later on.'

Marie opened up the present, which was a little figurine of a pony. Marie loved horses; her main present was five riding lessons.

I didn't know when I would be back, as the contract details were still being discussed – I would only get a formal contract after three months' successful employment, which I had not yet completed.

'Listen, kids,' I told them. 'Please be good for your Mum and do as you're told. I'll call you as often as I can.'

We were in Matthew's bedroom and were having one last cuddle before I left. Tears streaked all of our faces, and it broke my heart to hear Marie sobbing. Marie was my little girl and I had a bond with her that was very special. Matthew was as special to me, but I had brought him up to be more macho, which to my satisfaction was paying off.

Matthew was definitely fighting back the tears. He was going to miss me as much as I was going to miss him. We went everywhere together and did the boy things that Marie didn't want to do.

'Kevin is here!' called Anne.

'Okay kids,' I said, 'wave to me out of the window, and then go back to bed for a couple of hours – and don't forget to be good for your mum.' I knew it would be difficult saying goodbye to Anne, and it would be much more difficult if the kids were there.

Dad and Kevin packed my cases in the boot of the car and waited while me and Anne said our goodbyes.

'Don't worry, sweetheart. I'll be in touch often, and with any luck you can come out soon with the kids for a holiday.'

I got in the back of the car, and as we drove off I waved up at the kids, who had their faces pressed up against the glass with tears rolling down their faces. It was ten minutes before I gathered my composure and started to talk to Kevin and Dad.

'So, Dad, how do you fancy coming out to Abu Dhabi soon?' I said, breaking the silence.

'I should have an apartment soon, Dad. They told me that as soon as my three months is up they will sort one out, and I should have it by the end of January.'

'That's great, Rick. I'd love to come out and get away from this miserable winter weather. I'm not looking forward to staying in the mobile home for the rest of the winter, so any chance to get some sun on my back would be welcome.'

We discussed how difficult things were in the building industry, and other topics, on the way to the airport. Dad reassured me that he was feeling much better now that Christmas and New Year were out of the way, and his enthusiasm to visit Abu Dhabi and enjoy the sunshine brought much relief to me.

'Okay Rick, we are here,' said Kevin as he pulled up at the drop-off point. We had agreed that Kevin and Dad should head off as soon as they had dropped me off, as Kevin could still fit in his day's work if they headed straight back.

I thanked Kevin for the lift and we shook hands.

'That's okay Rick, glad I could help'

Kevin got back in the car and left Dad and I to say our goodbyes.

'Well, Dad I guess it'll be a month or two until I see you again, but I'll make arrangements for you to come out as soon as I have my apartment.'

'I'm looking forward to that, Rick. We'll be riding camels together before you know it!'

We both laughed, and as we hugged our eyes filled up. Not wanting to show his emotions, Dad quickly turned and got into the car.

I waved them off with tears streaming down my face. I was already missing Dad, and I felt guilty about having to go and work abroad, but my family depended on me and for now I had to follow the path that I had chosen.

*

The flight was uneventful, and it gave me the time to prepare myself mentally for the challenges ahead. I was collected at the airport by one of the sheikh's drivers, and although I was glad to be away from the winter weather back home, my mind often wandered back to the situation I had left behind. I checked into the hotel and had something to eat before going to bed.

I reported to the head office in the morning and met up with my boss Tony.

'Hello Rick, great to see you again,' said Tony. 'How are things back home?'

'Hello Tony, oh, not so bad, thanks, but I'm so glad that I went back to check it out for myself.'

Tony could hear the relief in my voice and knew that I was being sincere.

'It was a difficult time for my dad.' I gave Tony a summary of my visit home, but told him that I was looking forward to getting back to work.

'Well, I've got good news for you, Rick. You are going to be managing a renovation project of the sheikh's main palace and the marina where he keeps his speedboats and yachts.'

I was excited. I had always lived by the sea and spent many happy times windsurfing and water-skiing, so for me, being around boats was going to be the icing on the cake. I couldn't wait to tell Dad this extra news, he would be excited too.

I collected my company car and headed off straight to the marina, where I was to set up the site office in one of the empty marina buildings. I was introduced to some of the design team and a few of the foremen who would be reporting to me. Over the next three days I kept myself busy, planning the work and showing my boss, Tony, that I knew my stuff and that I would take my responsibilities head-on.

I phoned home every day, and was pleased that Dad had continued to stay with Anne and the kids since I left. On the fourth day Anne told me that Dad had gone but hadn't said where he was going.

'He's probably going to Elizabeth's or David's,' she told me.

'Why didn't you ask him where he was going before he left?' I said.

'I did ask him Rick, but he said he wasn't quite sure. He said he might go back to the mobile home.'

I knew that Dad hadn't been looking forward to going back to the mobile home. It was a very cold January.

'Do me a favour, darling,' I said, 'can you call Elizabeth, David and John and ask them if they have seen Dad? I'll call back tomorrow morning.'

Then I spoke to Matthew and Marie, whose voices I loved to hear. They were excited that I was working on a palace, and wanted to know all about it so they could tell their friends.

'Will you meet the prince and princess, Dad?' asked Marie excitedly.

'I don't know, sweetheart, but if I do I will tell them I have a prince and princess of my own.'

I phoned back the following morning as planned.

'Has anyone heard from Dad, Anne?'

'No, they haven't heard, but David is going to pop over to the mobile home later today. He's probably over there, or he may have gone to get the tug.' Anne was trying to defuse any worry that I might have built up. 'It's probably something simple like that, Rick. Try not to worry.'

I couldn't help but worry, after the events leading up to Christmas and what Dad had told me he would do if Mum died before him.

'Okay darling, I'll call tonight after work around six o'clock your time, but if you do hear from Dad, can you call head office and leave a message for me?'

My work phone had been set up so that it could not make international calls, so I couldn't call again until I had finished work and got back to the hotel. But before I finished work, I had a call from the secretary at head office, telling me that my wife wanted me to call home.

I drove down to the local shops, where there were public telephones, and bought a telephone card so I could make international calls.

'Hello' I said as Anne picked up the phone. My heart was pounding, and I was expecting Anne to say that Dad was at the mobile home or that he had been located somewhere else.

'Rick, did you get the news?'

'What news, Anne? Of course I haven't heard any news, how would I?'

'Your sister has been trying to get hold of you at the hotel.'

'So what *is* the news? Is Dad okay?'

A short silence was broken by the words I had dreaded and hoped I would never hear.

'Your Dad's been found dead at the mobile home.'

I heard the words, but my head went into a spin. I felt as though I was falling into an abyss and I could hear someone screaming as I fell to my knees.

As the phone hung there, swinging from side to side, Anne could hear me wailing and crying out, 'No! No! No!'

'Rick, are you there? Rick – please talk to me!' she cried.

I was on my knees and holding my head in my hands, shouting out, 'Why, Dad, why?'

People in the street stopped in their tracks when they heard my cries, and couldn't understand what was happening.

I was on my own and a long way from any friends or co-workers, unable to think rationally, and incapable of returning to the telephone. Suddenly I felt a hand on my shoulder, but I couldn't concentrate on anything but what was going on in my head.

*

'Are you okay sir?'

I was distraught, and it was a few minutes before I looked up at the man with the friendly voice but I couldn't focus on the detail of the man's face. A few people had gathered around by this point, and I knew I had to pull myself together.

'Sir, my name is Dr Yusuf. I live in an apartment across the street. Please come with me, I spoke to your wife on the phone, and she explained what happened. I told her you would call back soon. You can call from my apartment if you would like to.'

I couldn't hear what the man was saying. Dr Yusuf, the man who had put his hand on my shoulder, had been sitting outside a coffee shop close by, and had realized that the man he heard wailing and screaming must have received some tragic news over the phone. When he couldn't get a response from me, he picked up the phone, which was still swinging and had spoken to Anne. Dr Yusuf worked at the local hospital. He could see that I was in a severe state of shock, and as he knew now what had happened, he knew he had to let me settle at my own pace.

Dr Yusuf dispersed the small crowd, which was made up of local shop owners and a few shoppers. He helped me up from the floor and led me across the street to his apartment.

I was numb, happy to have someone take control of the situation. My head was still spinning, but the realization of what I had just been told was starting to sink in. The next thing I knew, I was in an apartment.

'Sit down there, Rick,' said Dr Yusuf, leading me to a big leather armchair. 'I will make some coffee.'

I sat leaning forward with my head in my hands, my head pounding as I tried to think straight.

'Here you are, Rick, drink this. It will make you feel better.'

I looked up at the doctor and could see that the man was ethnically either of Indian or Pakistani origin.

'My Dad is dead.' My voice was choked and low.

'I know, Rick. I spoke to your wife on the phone when I found you and she told me.'

I started to sob uncontrollably and was shaking violently.

'Come on, Rick. Try and drink some of this, it will really help you.'

Dr Yusuf had made a very sweet coffee, knowing that if he could get me to start drinking it, it would help to calm me down. It took over an hour for me to calm down enough to be able to tell the doctor how he could contact Anne and Tony, my boss. I couldn't face telephoning them. I knew I would just break down when I started to speak.

The doctor telephoned Anne and reassured her that I was safe and would be taken care of until arrangements could be made for me to return home. He then telephoned my head office and managed to get a message to Tony, who arrived twenty minutes later to take me to his own apartment.

'Thank you doctor, I'm sure Rick will be in touch to thank you just as soon as he can.'

Tony took me back to his plush penthouse, and told me he would make arrangements for me to fly home at the earliest opportunity. After a few hours, I asked to be taken to my hotel.

When I arrived at the hotel it was late in the evening. I told Tony that I would be fine and that I would call the office in the morning to find out what arrangements had been made and then made my way to my room on the tenth floor.

I had photographs of my family and of Mum on the wall above my bed. As soon as I saw them I collapsed on the bed in floods of tears. I felt so isolated and so alone; I just wanted to see my children and feel Anne's arms around me.

Before I got into bed I looked out of the window over the city of Abu Dhabi.

'Shall I just end it myself?' I said to myself as I opened the window. The very thought of how my children and Anne would feel made me physically sick.

I couldn't sleep that night, but I tried to focus on the fact I would be home within the next day or so.

23

A FAMILY IN SHOCK

Tony arranged everything for me; he sorted out a direct flight home for later on the following day, booked a car to take me to the airport and also had my belongings taken out of my hotel room and stored them at his own apartment.

I telephoned Anne and gave her the flight details and asked her to arrange for someone to collect me.

Tony had arranged for me to wait in the VIP lounge before boarding. He had told the airline about my situation and that I would not feel like talking to other travellers.

The flight was not full and I had a whole row of seats to myself on the Boeing 747. I told the flight attendants that I would not want any food on the seven-hour flight, and requested a blanket so that I could just try to sleep. I did manage to get some sleep, and before I knew it the captain announced that we would be landing in half an hour.

I hadn't brought any baggage with me, apart from a small holdall as I didn't want to have to wait at the baggage reclaim. I was very upset and was concerned that I would start crying at any moment. One of the flight attendants accompanied me off the plane and rushed me through passport control, ahead of other travellers.

As we left arrivals and emerged into the public area, Anne rushed forward and threw her arms around me. As we stood there sobbing and holding each other, it would probably have looked to bystanders and other travellers as though I had just returned from a long trip and that we were simply happy to see each other.

After a minute or two I managed to regain my composure, and turned round to see my good friend, Clive, standing there with his wife, Sue. I'd been friends with Clive ever since we'd met at school at the age of eleven. Now our children were around the same age, we often got together for family days out.

Anne had telephoned Clive and told him the news. She knew that as a lifelong friend, Clive would know what to say to me in my moment of despair.

I hugged Clive and he said simply, 'Don't worry, mate, everything will be fine.'

We were silent on the drive home. Anne did try to talk to me, but I was just lying on my back with my knees up with my head in her lap, staring up at her with tears streaming down the side of my face as I tried to make sense of things. I didn't know the cause of my dad's death at this point, but I knew that it was no accident.

We arrived at my house in the early hours. Clive and Sue said their goodbyes and drove off.

'The kids are at my mum's,' said Anne. 'I thought you'd need time to rest before you see them.'

'That was a good idea,' I said. 'I don't want them to see me all broken up like this; we'll get them tomorrow, once I have seen Elizabeth, John and David.'

We sat up for a couple of hours while Anne relayed as much detail as she had been able to gather. I was not surprised to hear that Dad had taken his own life by committing suicide in Mum's little car that John had given him back.

Anne had arranged for us to meet Elizabeth and my brothers at David's house the following afternoon. As we walked up the pathway to David's front door, he saw us from the kitchen window and rushed to open the door.

'Oh Rick, it's so good to see you,' he said as we met.

We hugged each other, and the feeling of grief overwhelmed us both. Anne continued into the house as we held each other and cried. Elizabeth and John greeted her.

'Where's Rick?' asked John quietly

'He's outside with David. They'll be in shortly.'

David and I entered the house soon afterwards and were greeted by Elizabeth and John. It wasn't long ago that we had all been together, celebrating the New Year, when we all had a group hug and told one and other that 'things could only get better'. We were concerned about Dad's welfare, but he had convinced us that although he was finding it difficult, he was coming to terms with the loss of his soul mate.

This time our group hug was very different. As we stood there with our arms around each other and our heads touching, we could not speak and in the silence our tears were dripping to the floor.

Anne and David's wife, Karen, were so moved by the situation that they were reduced to tears, and held each other in this awful moment of realization that we were left without our parents.

The fact that we were all grown up was irrelevant; here we were without the parents who had brought joy and laughter to our lives for so many years, and now it was all over.

After our initial period of open grief, we soon settled down to discuss what had to be done. David took responsibility of the formal arrangements for the forthcoming funeral. Elizabeth took control of all of the necessary paperwork and legal requirements while John and I took care of the personal effects at the mobile home and what needed to be concluded as far as the tug was concerned.

I found out that evening that it was David who had found Dad in the car, his face blackened with the fumes from the car exhaust. I could not have imagined being faced with that vision, but David seemed to me to be quite calm despite his ordeal, although I did not want to question him too deeply on it. David had always been very mature for his age, and even when Mum had died he dealt with it in a very dignified and personal way.

Although I felt much better after seeing my brothers and sister, I was really looking forward to seeing Matthew and Marie. At nine and eight respectively, they were just old enough to understand about life and death, but I didn't know whether were they old enough to understand suicide. Anne had told me that as far as the kids knew, their granddad had died and that was it. I knew that I had to be more explicit and thought very carefully about what I would have to say to them. They did not need to know the details of how their granddad had died, and as far as I was concerned the place and timing was not an issue at this stage.

The following day, Anne's parents brought the children back and left after a quick cup of tea. I spent some time with the children before trying to explain why I was home again.

'Do you remember when Nanny died?' I asked them.

'Yes, Dad,' replied Matthew with a knowing look.

'Well, Granddad loved Nanny so much that he couldn't live without her by his side.'

My eyes immediately filled with tears and I knew that it was having an effect on the children and Anne. I did not need to say anything else; the children knew instinctively what had happened even though they did not know the details.

Matthew and Marie understood the word 'suicide', as they had heard it mentioned over the past couple of months, but it meant nothing to them emotionally. Now they knew what suicide really meant, and as far as they were concerned their granddad had died of a broken heart.

As I looked into their eyes, I knew that I couldn't say anything that would explain why this had happened; the emotions that I felt were instantly picked up by the children, and they just sat on the settee and cuddled me without a word being said.

I was not the Dad who had left them just a few days earlier and had waved to them in the early hours on Marie's birthday.

The following days were consumed with funeral arrangements. Dad's brothers and sisters offered to do all they could, and there were many issues beyond the funeral arrangements that needed to be dealt with.

The funeral was a solemn affair, and in the circumstances it was not felt that his death should be celebrated in the same manner as Mum's. But the whole family did get together at the local pub where Dad used to drink, which had a function room, and he had a good send-off. Dad had been a very popular man amongst the family and neighbours where he used to live, and there were more than a hundred people at his funeral and his wake.

The days after the funeral took me into further misery when I found out that the boat brokers were holding the tug that Dad had virtually paid for because they wanted a further £5,000.

I visited the brokers with one of my uncles, and it was clear to me that they had deceived my dad on the contract. He had paid £18,000 and was due to pay a further £6,000, which he had budgeted for, but when we approached the brokers they wanted an additional £5,000 on top of the £6,000.

I had a copy of the original contract for £24,000, signed by my dad and the brokers, a company that represented a private seller.

'Your father agreed to pay us an additional £5,000 in cash,' the broker told me.

'Well, I'd say that would have been an illegal payment, wouldn't you?' I replied.

I was ready to try anything to conclude matters, but without having to pay the additional £5,000 that was being asked.

It took some hard bargaining, but in my time of woe the last thing that I wanted was a court battle over the tug, so we agreed to split the difference and I raised the £2,500 to release the tug. I had threatened to report the broker to the Inland Revenue if he stuck to his claim of £5,000 in cash.

A week later myself, my uncle and a hired hand collected the tug, paid the balance and delivered the tug to the local marina where Dad had originally planned to moor it while he prepared it for his journeys.

Elizabeth, my brothers and myself had discussed our Dad's estate, and a huge factor was the tug. None of us knew exactly what to do about it, but at least it was in our hands.

I was hoping to return to Abu Dhabi to pick up my career as a site manager, but when I telephoned my boss, Tony, to arrange my return to work, I was told that my services were no longer required as I was seen as someone who could not be relied on.

'It's not me, Rick,' Tony explained, 'It's the sheikh's adviser, Mohammed – he doesn't believe what you are saying.'

After all that I had been through, the last thing that I wanted to hear was that I was lying about my own father's death.

'Well, I have a return ticket, Tony, and I'll be back in two days as planned. I'll face Mohammed to explain things.'

I was prepared to fight for my position; I had nothing to lose now and returned to Abu Dhabi as planned. My hotel room had been cancelled, and Bob, who I had stayed with on my first visit, met me at the airport. The following day I went to see Tony, expecting my return to be met with some sympathy.

Tony soon made it clear that as far as the sheikh and his adviser were concerned, suicide was not something that they were comfortable with, and that they had no sympathy for me. Tony's hands were tied and he had been told to drop me. He tried to explain to me that the cultural differences were such that suicide was something that the Muslim society found intolerable.

I found it hard to accept that my commitment to my work and my unplanned return home had been so unacceptable. I pointed out that my father's suicide was an intolerable thing even in the Christian faith.

Tony tried hard to support me, but in the Arab States, expatriates are seen as an expendable commodity. 'Unless you are seen as someone who can bring money to the table,' he told me, 'your services are not worth an awful lot.'

I knew this was the end of the line and made arrangements to return home. Tony helped me with the cost of the flight home and was sad to see me go; he knew he had lost a good man who was struggling to cope with trying times at home.

I had no intention of trying to get another job in Abu Dhabi now. My energy had been sapped and I needed to be with Anne and the kids.

24

CONFIDENCE

I returned home in February 1993 and immediately decided to bring the tug up to a good enough condition to sell. Although Dad's estate was in probate, the solicitor managed to have some funds released so that I could pay the mooring fees and make arrangements to have some welding and other urgent repairs carried out.

Work was difficult to find. It was now March 1993 and the UK was in deep recession. I had to sign on for income support, which was something I hated to do. I was a proud man, but the wages that I had been offered to work for fell a long way short of covering my household outgoings. There were no government schemes at the time to assist in making up any shortfall.

I busied myself with cleaning the tug and making the necessary repairs. Now that the tug was seaworthy I decided that I could make it pay for itself while we sorted out the estate, if I took fishing parties out. I had plenty of friends who were interested in sea fishing, and for a small donation to cover the diesel and mooring cost I was taking fishing parties out every week.

Eventually Dad's estate was settled and Elizabeth, my brothers and I received a small amount of cash each. I advertised the tug, and by the end of the summer it was sold, which boosted my mood and confidence. I bought a small van, and started to undertake some private work that I managed to get through an advertisement I placed in the local paper, but this soon dried up as Christmas approached. The recession was still having a severe effect on the construction industry.

One evening, when I had been out with a friend at the local snooker hall, an elderly man approached us in a panicked state.

'Please help me,' he said. 'My friend has collapsed at the wheel and I don't know what to do.'

I could tell straight away that this was a serious situation, and instinctively took control.

'Paul, go and phone for an ambulance,' I told my friend.

The elderly man led me to the car, which was parked on a hill. As we approached, I could see a middle-aged woman slumped at the wheel.

It was a cold late November night, and as I opened the car door I could see that the woman was well wrapped up in a sheepskin coat. As I placed my ear to her mouth and felt her wrist for a pulse, I knew that she had stopped breathing. Thankfully I had been on many first aid courses at this point and so I knew what to do.

I pulled the woman from the car, released the buttons on her coat and started to apply mouth-to-mouth resuscitation.

The elderly man was looking on.

'Will she be all right?' he asked softly.

'She'll be fine,' I replied, between giving chest compressions and mouth-to-mouth resuscitation. Then, happening to blow too hard, I received a mouthful of the lady's stomach contents and then I could do no more, so I turned the woman onto her side and continued with the chest compressions as best I could.

The ambulance arrived after about five minutes, and the crew took over from me. I could see that they were using electroconvulsive equipment in the ambulance to try to revive the woman, but when the doors shut and the ambulance drove off I was certain that there was nothing they could do.

The following day, I visited the local hospital to find out what had become of the woman, and was not surprised to hear that she had died. I left my telephone number with the hospital and asked them whether they could pass it on to the woman's family, as I wanted to give them my condolences.

The phone rang a couple of days later.

'Hello?' I said as I answered it.

'Hello – can I speak to Rick, please?' said a soft voice.

'Speaking,' I said.

'My name is Maureen; I'm the daughter of the lady you tried to save, and I just wanted to thank you for your efforts.'

I didn't know what to say; I knew only too well what the family were going through. My eyes filled with tears and at first I was unable to speak. But I composed myself and managed a few words.

'Is it okay if I come and see you? I would like to speak to you.'

'Of course it is, Rick. My brothers and me would love to meet you.'

I took down the address, and made my way over to see Maureen and her brothers the following day.

'Hi, Rick, please come in,' said Maureen after I had introduced myself.

I could feel the sadness in the house; it was the sadness I had felt earlier in the year. I was introduced to Maureen's three brothers, who all wanted to thank me for trying to save their mother's life.

As the details came out about the woman I had tried to save, I found it all very coincidental. Her name was Rose; she had three sons and one daughter, and she was the same age as my own mother when she died.

'My mum believed in life after death,' said Maureen, 'and she will no doubt thank you herself some time.'

I had an open mind to such things, so I didn't dismiss what Maureen had said. I hadn't planned to tell her about my own parents, but it came out and I became very upset. Maureen and her brothers were interested in what I had to say, and they too found it interesting that there were so many coincidences.

'I'm sorry,' I said, 'I didn't want to bring my parents' deaths up, but I did want you to know that I totally understand how you feel right now.'

The five of us in various states of being upset felt very close to each other, and I asked if I could attend the funeral. Maureen and her brothers were only too happy to have me there.

'My mum will be looking down on you, Rick, and will help you in your hour of need,' said Maureen as she saw me to the door.

'Thanks Maureen. I'll bear that in mind.'

At the funeral I was more shocked than ever when the same hymns were sung that were played at my mum's funeral. I went back to the house for the wake and was thanked by many of the family for trying so hard to save her life.

This was a difficult time for me, I was struggling to pay the bills and although I had sent my CV to several agencies, I wasn't getting any positive responses. Not only was there no work at all as Christmas day approached, but I was also feeling very depressed, as the anniversary of Dad's death was just three weeks away.

Just a few days before Christmas, the telephone rang. I answered without any enthusiasm for anything and presumed it was one of my family members calling.

'Hello is that Rick?' said a voice at the other end of the phone.

'Yes, this is Rick.'

'My name is Mike. I'm a consultant for a recruitment company, and I found your CV on our files. I'd like to know if you'd be interested in working in the Middle East?'

I immediately got excited – a positive call for a change.

'Yes, I'd like to meet up with you to discuss things, Mike.'

'Can you come to London tomorrow for an interview? This is a post I want to get filled urgently. I can't tell you too much over the phone, as it's a high-profile project.'

'Okay Mike, just tell me where to come and what time, and I'll be there.'

As I wrote down the address, I couldn't wait to tell Anne. I was unsure how she would feel about me working abroad again, but knew I had to try. I gave her the few details that I had been given as soon as she got home from shopping.

'Of course you should go, if the opportunity is there, Rick. After all, the opportunities are not here, are they?'

Anne had always supported me in the things I had done; I was a good provider and only had my family's interests at heart.

I arrived at the offices of the recruitment company the following day and met Mike. During the interview, Mike told me that the position was for a project manager on a palace for a high-ranking prince in Saudi Arabia.

Mike was happy with me, and told me that he would forward my CV and interview results to the construction manager in Saudi Arabia and would try to get me an answer within the next couple of days.

I didn't move very far from the phone for those two days, and every time it rang I hoped it would be Mike.

'I'm sorry, but I'm waiting for a call,' I would tell anyone who phoned.

By the third day I was starting to feel despondent, and wondered whether I should call Mike, but Anne told me to wait one more day. The next day would be Christmas Eve, and I was sure that I had not been selected for the job.

On Christmas Eve the telephone rang at midday. I didn't think for a moment that it would be Mike.

'Hello?' I said as I picked up the phone.

'Hello Rick, it's Mike here. Happy Christmas.'

'Oh, hi, Mike. Happy Christmas to you.'

'Well, Rick, it's good news and bad news, I'm afraid.'

I didn't know what to think, and just responded with 'I'll have the bad news first, if that's okay with you.'

'Well Rick, the bad news is that you'll need to come to London today with your passport, so that I can start to process your paperwork.'

'Oh, my God! Are you serious?'

I was so excited that I didn't think to ask what the good news was.

'Do you want the good news now, then, Rick?'

'Of course, of course. Sorry – I'm just so happy.'

'Well, Rick, I've secured you a six-month contract, and you'll have your own apartment with a shared swimming pool.'

There were a few seconds' silence.

'Well, Mike, you've just given me the best Christmas present I could have wished for.'

'Okay Rick, just get yourself up here. I need your passport to arrange the sponsorship. You're leaving in two weeks.'

'I'll be with you in a couple of hours, Mike. See you soon.'

I hung up the phone and desperately searched for my passport. Eventually I found it in a box that Anne kept all our important and personal documents in. Anne was out doing some last-minute shopping with the children, so I left a message to say that I had to go to London and would be back in a few hours. I wanted to tell Anne to her face about the job.

It took four hours for me to drive to London and back, and I had not felt so excited for a long time. I knew this was only going to be a six-month contract, but it would give me the chance to get more experience of working abroad which was so important to companies seeking British managers.

When I arrived home, Anne was preparing the evening meal.

'Well Anne it's on. I'm going to Saudi Arabia in two weeks' time.

'Oh, Rick, that's great news,' Anne said in her usual supportive way.

She was really pleased for me. She had seen me become depressed with the work situation in the UK, and when I was depressed I was prone to drinking too much, which compounded our financial problems.

Christmas and New Year passed by with a new spring in my step.

I had been dreading the New Year and always felt as though I was letting my family down by not having a good job. Now things were going to be different, and although I knew it would be difficult being away from my family again, I knew that I had no choice.

This opportunity had arrived at just the right time and I couldn't help thinking of what Maureen had told me about her Mum. 'My mum will be looking down on you, Rick, and will help you in your hour of need.'

I could feel myself thinking that perhaps there was more to life.

*

I left for Saudi Arabia just a few days after Marie's ninth birthday, and although many tears were shed, I told my family 'it was all for the best,' and I believed it was.

The first couple of weeks were difficult for me. I felt homesick and was working twelve hours a day, six days a week. I had to drive 100 kilometres each way from my apartment to the palace, which was out in the desert. I wished I had asked more about the details of the job, but in my heart I knew I would have still taken it. The contract said I would be working forty-eight hours a week, but I didn't want to rock the boat by sticking to the contract. I was actually working seventy-two hours a week with twelve hours' driving on top of that. I was promised a bonus if I got the job done on time, and though the amount of the bonus was never specified I put every effort into my work.

One thing that always motivated me about large construction projects was the range and scope of things that needed to be done; from the initial paperwork, to setting out the groundwork and then finally seeing the high class finishing of the project. Nothing gave me more pleasure, and a new project was just what I needed.

At the end of the six months, I had delivered the project on time and to budget, and was told that I could have a few days off before returning to the UK. Nothing was said about the promised bonus, so I decided to speak to Peter, one of the directors, who had made the promise. He called me into the head office just two days before I was due to go home.

A secretary directed me into Peter's plush office.

'Hello Peter,' I said, 'can I have a word with, you please?'

'Hello Rick. What can I do for you?'

I got straight to the point, as I knew that Peter would have to discuss the matter with the other two directors.

'It's about the bonus you promised me if I got the job done on time, which I feel I've managed to do...'

'You certainly did, Rick, and we've discussed your bonus, but we want to know what you think your bonus should be.'

I felt that I had been put in a very awkward position and one that was unfair.

'I'll have to think about that Peter. I'll come back in two hours with my thoughts, if that's okay with you.'

'Sure, Rick. I look forward to seeing you then.'

I left the office and went back to my apartment. As a professional project manager, I had recorded all the hours that I had worked in my site diary, and decided that I would calculate how many hours I had worked over and above those required by my contract and suggested that this should be a starting-point for my bonus. I was surprised to find that the hours were equivalent to an additional two months' pay, and didn't think that Peter would agree to that, let alone any more.

'Hello Peter,' I said as I re-entered the office just two hours later.

After I had explained how I had calculated the figure, Peter told me to return the following day at the same time, when he would have spoken to the other directors.

The following day, I went back to the office feeling very nervous. I felt that I should at the very least receive an extra two months pay' in addition to any bonus, but in truth I would have been satisfied with just one month's pay.

'Well, Rick, I've spoken to the other directors, and we have agreed with your figures. We know the effort you have put in, and the Prince is very happy with the palace.'

I was staggered. I had expected that I would have had to negotiate on the figure.

'Furthermore, Rick,' Peter continued, 'we're going to pay you an additional two weeks on top of that, to show you our gratitude for your efforts.'

I was lost for words. Just a few hours earlier I was planning my argument for what I thought was reasonable, and here I was being offered so much more.

'Call in tomorrow, Rick, and I'll have the cash here waiting for you.'

All transactions were carried out in cash and this included the wages for the 400 men who had worked on the site during the project. I knew it was oil money, and that in Saudi Arabia the saying was "Cash is king".

I collected my money on the day I was due to leave Saudi Arabia, and was concerned about the amount of cash I would have to take through customs.

I had been joined in Saudi Arabia six weeks before the end of the project by Stan, my best mate who I had managed to arrange a job for as the supervisor for some of the finishing on the external work around the palace grounds.

Stan agreed to help me secrete the cash amongst our belongings, which included hiding the cash in a guitar and in the lining of our suitcases.

We were really worried as the amount that we were allowed to take out in cash was equivalent to £400, and here we were trying to take out over £8,000.

Everything worked out well, and we were not searched at either of the airports on our return home.

I had suggested to Anne that she plan a fortnight's holiday to the Canary Islands. I really needed a break after working six days a week for six months solid without a break, and I knew that I needed to spend two weeks with just Anne and the kids.

During my work in Saudi Arabia I had enjoyed some memorable times, but deep down my thoughts were always on my family, and I don't think a week went by without at least one night where I cried myself to sleep thinking about being with Anne and the kids.

PART SEVEN:

MY STRUGGLE

25

MY NAME'S RICK AND I'M AN ALCOHOLIC

After the holiday in the Canaries, I cleared our debts with my bonus money, and bought a small van to start working as a builder again. I applied for site manager jobs but my stint in Saudi Arabia was not working in my favour. I had decided that missing my wife and children was far too difficult for me to go back out there to look for work again. The holiday in the Canaries had taught me that my kids needed their dad around to build memories and have some good fun with.

'Potential employers will see you as a risk,' one of the employment agency consultants told me, 'They'll think that if you were offered a lucrative contract abroad, you would just give your notice and go.'

There was some truth in what the consultant had said, and I knew that I had to try to start my own business again. Just as before, I found it difficult to find work; there was so much competition that I was being told I was too dear. I hadn't overpriced the jobs I did get, but I had no accounts with suppliers so I'd had to pay top prices for materials. The only way I could get the best discounts and open an account was to spend regularly with the suppliers to show them I was reliable. It was a catch-22 situation, and I soon found myself becoming depressed again. I started to drink again, and before very long this was causing problems between Anne and me.

I found that drinking took my mind off of the hurt and sadness. I would often come home just as Anne was going to bed and although she was never aggressive with her words or her actions, anything she said to try to get me to see reason made me angry and that's when the arguments would start.

'I have to go down the pub,' I told Anne, 'That's where business is done.'

I used any excuse to go to the pub. I couldn't see that the drink was obscuring my rational thoughts, but one thing was for sure: I felt ashamed that I was unable to provide for my family as I had done in previous years.

Over the next couple of years, my relationship with Anne deteriorated and my drinking escalated. I knew I was losing my wife, and our inability to communicate was starting to affect the children.

Matthew and Marie could see what was going on, but they never voiced their views. They loved us and had been brought up to respect us and not question anything. The kids would often cry themselves to sleep after hearing their mother and I arguing or – more to the point – me saying awful things to Anne that I would never have said to her when sober, even in my wildest dreams.

I eventually decided to leave Anne, despite the fact that I loved her dearly. I could not see that it was my drinking and my constant mood swings that were the heart of our problems. A lot of our other issues stemmed from my drinking, and it was no wonder that she didn't find me sexually attractive anymore, I was usually too drunk and couldn't even see the point of taking pride in myself.

*

I spent the next four years in various states of depression and never managed to hold down a job for very long. I became preoccupied with thoughts about avenging Hugh again, and found myself planning new acts of vengeance, which I carried out about every two months.

These acts were much as before. I would cause damage to Hugh's car and smash his windows, and more letters were put through Hugh's neighbours' doors to remind them that they lived close to a paedophile.

My drinking had reached new heights, and several of my family and friends were becoming concerned for my health. I had put on about three stone and could often be found unconscious on the floor as a result of too much alcohol.

One year I invited my brothers, sister, children and a few good friends to a Christmas party, and by ten o'clock that evening I was literally under the table behaving in a ridiculous manner that I thought was funny, and I became very angry when everyone started to leave.

'Okay, it's your loss,' I told them as I showed the last person out of the door.

I woke up the following morning and couldn't even remember what had happened. I knew that my brothers and sister had left early and had told me that I was drinking too much, but I was in denial.

My best friend, Stan, who had attended the party, called in to see me later that day and was not surprised to see me suffering from a severe hangover.

'Rick,' he said, 'we have known each other for a long time, and I'm worried about how much you're drinking.'

I listened, but although I knew that what was being said was true, I tried to make excuses.

'No more excuses, Rick,' said Stan. 'Your brothers and sister have been in contact with me and have asked me to talk to you, so you either listen to me or we will be falling out.'

Stan and I had grown up together, and this was a serious wakeup call. My family might have expressed their concern, but to be told by my best friend that he would fall out with me if I didn't address my drinking was worrying. I knew Stan meant it, whereas I knew my family would not be prepared to disown me.

'I will leave you to think about what I said, Rick,' Stan told me, 'and I just hope you see sense.'

Later in the day, Elizabeth called round to see me, and asked me to accompany her and my brothers to the cemetery to place some flowers on our parents' grave.

I knew that there would be an awkward moment when I got in the car, but before I could apologize for my behaviour the previous night, Elizabeth started to tell me why they were really there.

'Rick, we're going to the cemetery to put flowers on Mum and Dad's grave, and we're concerned that it won't be too long before it's your grave we are visiting, too.' Elizabeth was looking at me with a very serious look on her face, which was not something I could ever remember seeing before. 'If you don't get a grip of your drinking and seek help it will kill you; do you understand that?'

I looked at John and David, who were sitting in the back seat of the car, in the hope that I might get some support, but they just looked at me with stern faces.

'Elizabeth's right, Rick,' said David. 'You're a mess. What do you think Mum and Dad would say if they could see you now?' He hated saying that to me, but it was true, I *was* a mess, and the mention of what our mum and dad might think did strike a nerve.

'Okay, I will get some help, I promise you.' I knew I had to do something about my drinking, and by making a promise to my siblings I had also made the promise to my Mum and Dad.

We continued to the cemetery and placed the flowers on the headstone as planned. I became very emotional and told myself that I had to try hard to stop drinking.

I did cut down on my intake of alcohol, but failed to stop completely. Within three months, I was back to drinking as heavily as before, but managed to hide it from my family and friends by having less contact with them.

I was working as a site manager and Colin, a painting contractor, commented on my drinking problem. Colin had seen the signs. My breath always had a whiff of alcohol about it, and I would always have a drink at lunchtime. My eyes were often bloodshot and I would look dishevelled at meetings.

'You need to get hold of your drinking problem, Rick,' Colin told me in a friendly manner.

'Who said I have a problem?' I retorted defensively.

'I can see it Rick. I used to have a problem, but I have not had a drink now for five years, and my life is so much better for it.'

I found it very coincidental that Colin had commented on my drinking shortly after my own siblings had expressed their serious concerns.

'If you ever need any help, just call me, Rick. I have contacts in Alcoholics Anonymous who can help you.'

I dismissed his comments at first and thanked him for his concern but assured him that I was fine.

I knew that I had a serious decision to make, but I didn't know where to go for help, so that evening I decided to call Colin to see what he could suggest. After all, I had made a promise to my siblings and my deceased parents three months earlier and I wanted to keep it.

'Hi, it's Rick here,' I told Colin over the phone. 'I'd like to take you up on your offer to help me with my drink problem.' I now fully accepted that I had a serious problem that I could not deal with on my own.

'Okay, Rick, give me your address, and I'll have someone pick you up in an hour or so.'

I gave him my address, and as planned there was a knock on the door within the hour. It was about seven o'clock on a Friday night, and I had no idea who was at the door or where I was going.

'Hi, you must be Rick,' said the tall man as I opened the door. 'I'm Phil, I believe you're expecting me.'

'Yes, I am, but that's all I know.'

'We are going to an Alcoholics Anonymous meeting, and hopefully it will be the start to your recovery.'

Phil looked like a hard man who had worked in the sun for years. His face was weathered, and with his bald head, he had the look of a night club bouncer.

When we got into Phil's car, there was another man in the passenger seat, and after initial introductions we were off to the meeting.

The two men in the front seats chatted between themselves, but although I wanted to ask questions, I felt very nervous and decided to wait and see where they were taking me.

After half an hour, we arrived at a small hall. The three of us entered and were met by some friendly people. It was clear to me that almost everyone knew each other and that this was a very well-organised meeting.

After the initial introductions, the eighteen assembled people sitting in a circle were invited to speak, and with the usual, 'My name is —, and I am an alcoholic.' The first person started to speak and told the others how she had struggled that week to not have a drink, but that with the help of her sponsor (a fellow alcoholic) she had managed to get through.

I found the whole thing very moving, as some of the people who were invited to speak were reduced to tears as they told of their reasons for becoming alcoholics and how difficult it was to remain sober.

Eventually I was asked by the chairman for the night if *I* wanted to speak, but was told I didn't have to speak if I didn't want to.

'It's great that you have had the courage to come here, Rick, and that is the first step; so don't feel that you have to say anything just yet.'

I thought about it and decided to speak. I had listened to the others' stories and had picked up on the opening line that was the custom.

'Hello my name is Rick, and I am an alcoholic.' I found it strange to tell a room full of strangers that I was an alcoholic, and had not planned for the occasion, so what I said was purely off the cuff. 'This is my first visit to AA, and I suppose I should start by explaining why I think I became an alcoholic.'

I immediately thought back to when my mum died, and that triggered thoughts of my dad's suicide.

'My mum died suddenly in 1991 and as a result of that—' I broke down in tears and within a matter of seconds I was sobbing uncontrollably.

The room remained totally silent and my crying triggered one or two people to start crying too.

I felt a hand on my shoulder.

'Do you want to stop, Rick? There's plenty of time to let it out.'

I composed myself as much as I could, and was determined to continue.

'I had never considered why my drinking became so serious,' I said quietly. My head was in my hands and I could barely see through the tears that were forming a puddle on the wooden floor. 'I now know that I need to find out what has caused me to rely so much on drink, and I hope that coming to AA will help me to deal with it.' I was staring at the floor. 'I'm sorry for crying, but this is so difficult for me.' I started to cry again.

'Okay, Rick. One thing you don't need to do is apologize, you are amongst friends now, and we'll be here to help whenever you need us.'

A woman sitting next to me put her arm on my shoulder and said, 'Well done, Rick.'

As I looked up and wiped my eyes, I felt an atmosphere of sincere warmth and friendship that I had not felt for a long time.

The meeting was so enlightening for me that I knew that I had to attend as many meetings as possible in order to remain sober. Phil had told me on the way home that he would pick me up every night if I was prepared to attend other meetings.

I took Phil up on his offer, and over the next few weeks I attended AA every night and also at the weekends. Eventually I started to attend the meetings on my own, and started to make many more friends. I still broke down in tears when I told of what I felt had contributed to my drinking, and in particular when I spoke of what my mum suffered at the hands of Hugh; it really did have an effect on me.

One evening at a meeting, a kind, elderly man suggested to me that I might benefit from writing down my innermost thoughts as a way of clearing them from my mind.

'I'll try that,' I told him as I left the meeting, and thanked him for his advice.

26

ACTS OF REVENGE RESURFACE

As time went on, I continued to write down my thoughts and attend AA, and although I managed to stop drinking, I opened up more about what was behind my reasons for drinking.

The problem was bigger than me, and although my relationship with Matthew and Marie had never really faltered, I knew that they were worried about me and I had to stay sober for them. I was also conscious about how Anne felt and what I had put her through. I knew that whatever happened, we should remain good friends.

I still loved Anne, and I knew at the time, that even if she was prepared to have me back, it probably wouldn't have worked.

I was surprised at how much I was writing down in the book that I had bought specifically to document my feelings.

My desire and need to persecute the man who had brought so much misery to my mother occupied my thoughts more than anything.

I wrote down my innermost thoughts and realized that Hugh's actions all those years ago were responsible for my own mental instability.

The more I attended AA, the more my confidence and my need to persecute Hugh grew. I eventually decided to confront Hugh, and planned to visit my so-called granddad on the pretext of wanting to cement long-lost relationships. My real reason was to collect all of the photographs that Hugh had of my mum as a child, no matter what I had to do to get them.

I asked my brother, David, whether he would be prepared to accompany me on the visit.

'I'll come,' David told me, 'but I don't want any trouble.'

'All I want to do is collect the photographs of Mum that he has, and I'm sure that if we can persuade him to let us in, he will get them out.'

My plan was simple and required confidence and nothing else.

We approached the front door. It was late afternoon and still light. I rang the bell, and within a few seconds I could see through the obscured glass that someone was approaching the door.

'Hello – can I help you?' said a middle-aged woman as she opened the door.

I did not recognise her, but I had made enquiries and knew that Hugh still lived at the address.

'Hello' I replied. 'Is Hugh in?'

Before the woman could say another word the door opened further and Hugh was standing there before David and me.

'Hello Granddad. It's Rick and David, your grandsons.'

Hugh's face turned white and he pushed the door closed without a word being said. I had been ready for this reaction and put my foot in the door in anticipation.

'Granddad, what's the matter? We've come round to see you, to find out how you are and tell you about your great-grandchildren.'

I pushed the door open. Hugh was unsure what to do or say and reluctantly let us into the hallway.

'What's going on, Hugh?' said the woman. It was clear that Avril was either dead or no longer with Hugh.

'Sorry, I don't know who you are,' I told the woman, but we are Hugh's grandsons and we have only just found out where he lives. We lost contact years ago when we were young.

The woman was convinced by what I was saying, and Hugh had not put up any further resistance.

'We wanted to let Nan and Granddad know they had great-grandchildren, that's all.'

'Yes, Hugh has spoken about you all, and I have seen photographs of you when you were younger,' said the woman who was not Avril. She seemed confused, and looked at Hugh for some sort of explanation.

'It's nice to see you Rick,' said Hugh. 'How have you been?' He sounded nervous and not at all interested in how David and me were.

'We're all okay, Granddad.'

I knew that Hugh always had photographs of our Mum on the fireplace and windowsills, taken at bird shows that she was forced to enter when she was a teenager. I could remember the look on Mum's face in those photographs, and they were not looks of joy and happiness.

The four of us were still standing in the hallway, and there was an uncomfortable feeling in the air.

'Do you have the photographs of Mum with the rosettes when she won the bird show competitions Granddad? I'd love to see them again.'

'Yes, they are in the living room, I'll go and get them.'

Hugh returned straight away with a large photograph of our Mum holding a huge rosette with 'FIRST' written across the middle.

I took the photo out of Hugh's hand and looked at it with tears starting to collect in my eyes.

'Yes, that's the one I was hoping to see,' I said as I held the photograph.

I looked at David, who was starting to feel that things were not going as he had expected. He knew me well and that there was no way I would leave without at least that one photograph.

I looked at the unknown woman, who still seemed somewhat bemused by the unfolding conversation.

'Do you know who this is in the photograph?' I asked her.

'Yes, Hugh often talks about Rose and how special she was to him.'

I knew now that I would have to change my initial plan to get the photographs by an agreeable method.

'Did Hugh, my so-called granddad, ever tell you what he made my mum do to him and what he did to her when she was a child?' As I uttered those words I looked her in the eye and pointed at Mum and Hugh in the photograph.

Hugh tried to snatch the photograph out of my hand, but the old man was no match for me.

'I'm calling the police!' shouted Hugh, reaching for the telephone on the small table in the hallway.

'No, you're not, Hugh,' I retorted as I kicked the phone off the table and pulled the cable from the wall socket.

'Rick, you said you wouldn't cause any trouble!' yelled David, trying to pull me out of the front door.

I had no intention of harming anyone, and as Hugh made his way to the front door saying that he was going to get his neighbour, I just said, 'Go get them, they know what you are.'

David left the property, telling me that he was not prepared to get arrested.

I was left alone with the unknown woman. She was probably fifteen to twenty years younger than Hugh, and although I did not have a clue who he she was, I didn't really care.

'My so-called Granddad mistreated my mum from the age of three until the age of sixteen, did he tell you that?' The woman was dumbstruck, but something in her eyes told me that she believed what I was saying, or that she had reasons not to disbelieve it.

Three men entered the door within a few minutes of Hugh's leaving.

'What do you think you're doing, mate?' said the first as he approached me.

'I'm just collecting what's mine that's all.'

'Rick! What are you doing here?' said a second man with a shocked look on his face.

I had gone to school with him, and although I didn't remember his name, I did recognize him.

'My wife is calling the police. Why don't you just get out of here before they get here.'

'I've got nothing to hide, and as it happens, I have something to tell them, so I'll wait outside and speak to them when they arrive.'

I took the photograph with me and sat on the garden wall opposite the house.

I dropped the photo behind the wall with the intention of retrieving it the next day.

Within a couple of minutes three police cars and a dog unit arrived at the property.

I wondered what Hugh had been telling his neighbours. I was sure that had I been robbing a bank, the police wouldn't have turned up so quickly and in such numbers.

As I sat on the wall watching the police and neighbours looking over in my direction, the police did not come to talk to me at first, and this made me curious, but eventually a WPC and a male officer approached me.

'So what has been going on here then, sir?'

'Nothing, officer. I decided to ask my granddad for the photos of my mum, who is dead as a result of what he did to her.'

After I had tried to explain things, one officer said, 'If you have proof of what he has done, or any evidence, then you need to seek legal advice, not take things into your own hands.'

'I've done nothing, officer, and if my granddad wants to take me to court for anything, then I'll be happy to attend, and I'll tell the court why I was here.'

At this the policemen went back to Hugh's house. After ten minutes or so they returned and told me that Hugh did not want to take any action. They said I was free to go, but that they would need to speak to me over some other issues within the next few days.

I knew exactly what they were referring to. Perhaps after all these years of not knowing, Hugh had at last realized who had been vandalising his property and who had caused him so much inconvenience and heartache.

The following day, I went back to where I had dropped the photo behind the garden wall, but it had gone. I knocked on the door to find out whether the homeowner had taken the photo in.

'I'm sorry,' she told me, 'but I was watching out of the window yesterday, and I saw you drop the photo in our garden; and when you had gone I called over to see Hugh, as I thought it had something to do with him. He told me it was his, so I gave it back.'

I gave a brief explanation of the events of the day before and the woman was very apologetic.

'Not to worry,' I said, 'Hugh will be haunted by that photo until he dies.'

I then left, but not before I had reminded the woman that Hugh had mentally and sexually abused my mother when she was a child.

Two weeks after David and I visited Hugh, I was at home one evening, preparing to go to an AA meeting, when there was a knock at the door.

'Hello can I help you?' I said as I opened the door to the two policemen standing on the doorstep.

'Are you Mr Joyce?'

'Yes, I am,' I replied

'May we come in, please?'

'Of course.'

I led the police officers into the living room.

'We have had several complaints from your grandfather, Mr Harris, over many years about some very serious acts of vandalism, including his windows being broken on several occasions.'

The first policeman looked at me for a reaction, but I just sat there and stared back at them.

'How can I help you, then?' I asked calmly.

'Do you have any knowledge of who may be responsible for these acts?' came the reply from the second officer.

'Why would I know anything?'

'You were recently involved in a situation where the police were called as a result of you trying to obtain photographs from your grandfather's property. As a result of this we have decided to open up the files of his complaints, and would like to know if you were responsible for any of the following complaints.'

The policeman read out more than thirty-five complaints, from abusive telephone calls to attacks on Hugh's property.

'I'm afraid I can't help you, officer.' I knew that the officers were sure that I was responsible for the attacks, but without any evidence I was safe. I knew that my acts of revenge would have to stop now, as I assumed that after this recent event, Hugh would have put two and two together.

'We'll be making some further enquiries, and may need to speak to you again, Mr Joyce, but please let us know if you hear anything about the attacks on your grandfather.'

The police officers left, and I went off to the AA meeting feeling very good. I never felt guilty about the things that I had done to Hugh, and only wished that I had done more.

Two days after the police officers' visit, I received a letter from Hugh's solicitor, enclosing a court order for me to keep away from Hugh's property by half a mile or risk prosecution. I laughed at the letter, and although I had no plans to visit Hugh again, either to get photographs or to cause damage, I often drove past Hugh's property just for fun.

27

A GUN

I continued my visits to AA, and as time went on I became slimmer and more focused on my work. I started my own business as a health and safety adviser to small building companies, and I prepared a training course for site managers. If there was one thing I knew about more than anything, it was how to run building projects, and I wanted to share that knowledge.

During this period, my relationship with Anne was starting to get better and I had always met my financial commitments as far as the kids were concerned.

Matthew had come to live with me for a short period, but Marie remained with Anne. I had always been very close to Matthew and we missed each other's company a great deal. It reminded me of my own relationship with my dad, which had its ups and downs, but I was determined that Matthew and me would be friends forever.

I had never felt so good, and as the months went on, I began to feel that I could do anything I wanted. Some of my family and friends were worried that I had changed so much, so quickly. I had lost weight and looked like a different man. Although my family were happy that I was getting better and not drinking, it was clear something was not quite right.

Clive, one of my closest friends who had collected me from the airport when I returned from Saudi Arabia, even asked me if I had cancer, such was his concern at my weight loss.

'It's not me who has the problem Clive,' I said, 'take a look at yourself in the mirror, you need to lose some weight'.

My confidence was beyond anything they had seen, and sometimes they couldn't understand my behaviour.

As I was no longer drinking, I drove my friends to a night club in my new Jaguar. We pulled up outside a night club and parked on double yellow lines.

Excuse me, sir, I'm afraid you can't park there,' came a deep voice as me and my friends approached the club entrance.

'Pardon me?' I said as I squared up to the heavily set doorman.

'I said you can't park there,' came the response.

'And what are you, then? A fucking traffic warden?'

My friends immediately stepped in.

'Come on, Rick. Just move the car. We don't want any trouble, do we.'

I calmly got into the car, moved it to a parking bay and walked back to the club.

'What the hell was that all about, Rick?' asked one of my friends. They were concerned for me, as I didn't appear to be at all nervous about approaching the doorman, who was a huge man.

'What do you mean? He's a doorman, not a traffic warden. I can park where I want, can't I?'

The night out continued without further incident. When I had dropped my friends off home, I decided to drive around town and watch the antics of the people wandering the streets in the early hours of the morning. When I looked at the drunks and how they were behaving, I realized that I was looking at how I used to behave not so long ago. I had been sober for about eleven months and I felt that I was in full control of my mind and body. I knew now that if I wanted to become successful again, I would have to keep sober.

This did not mean that my quest for vengeance was in any way reduced, and as I drove around I had an overwhelming desire to go to Hugh's house and knock on the door to ask for the photographs of Mum. In the end, I decided to drive home and plan something very different for Hugh.

The following day I called a close friend who apparently had access to guns.

'Hi Gary, it's Rick here,' I said as Gary answered the phone.

Gary was a long-term drinking friend of mine, who was known for dealing drugs and had always said that, if needed, he could get

a gun for friends. I had always thought it was just beer talk, as did most of the others that Gary had told.

'Hi, Rick, how's it going, mate?' We had not seen each other for a couple of years, but we had spent some good times together in the past.

'Yeah, things are good, thanks,' I said. 'I need a big favour, mate. Is it possible to meet up with you and have a chat?'

'Sure thing, Rick. Let's meet down the boatyard later – say about five thirty?'

I hung up after chatting about old times, and looked forward to our meeting.

'So, Rick, what have you been up to? I hear you're off the beer now.'

'Yeah, I've sorted myself out, and things are good, but I have a score to settle and...' I paused for a second, 'I need a handgun.'

'Holy shit, Rick.' Gary was visibly shocked. I had always been a bit of a lad, but had always kept the villainous guys and drug pushers at arm's length. Gary could hear in my voice that I was serious.

'Well, I can get a gun for you, but it won't be cheap, mate. It'll cost you at least a couple of grand.'

'That's fine, Gary, I can cover that. When can you get it?'

'About a week, and needless to say, Rick, it's yours to get rid of once you're done with it. Don't keep it, for God's sake.'

The arrangements were made, and as planned, I collected the gun the following week along with ten bullets. Gary didn't ask any questions. He didn't want to know who the victim was going to be.

I went home and put the gun and the bullets in the draw. There was nothing complicated about the gun. Gary had explained how to load it and had shown me how the safety catch worked.

Hugh was going to die the next day, and I felt elated about that, but for the first time in a long time, I felt nervous.

'What am I doing?' I asked myself.

I knew that what I was planning was not right. I also knew that I would probably get caught. I knew that the police would soon be knocking on my door if I went through with it.

After a full assessment, Dr Jarrod, a well-respected psychiatrist, suggested that I might be having manic phases, and told me that he wanted to put me on a course of drugs.

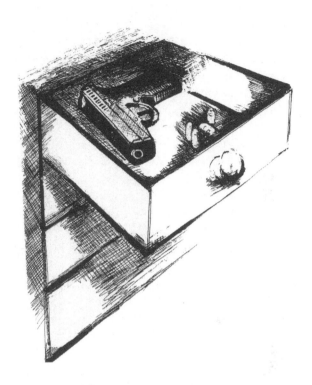

I contacted my doctor the following day and made an appointment. I knew I needed some professional advice. Although I had never felt so good, I also knew that planning to kill Hugh was one thing, but actually doing it was totally wrong and would mean that I could be locked up.

I kept my appointment and explained all that had happened, and although I held back from owning up about the gun, I did tell the doctor that I wanted to kill Hugh.

The doctor listened with interest, and after making a quick phone call he offered me some immediate help.

'I'm going to refer you to the mental health unit, Rick. Can you get there tomorrow to see Dr Jarrod?'

'Sure, doctor, that's not a problem.'

I took down the details and attended the mental health unit as planned.

I wasn't keen on taking drugs, but something inside me told me to trust the doctor and do as I was told. I disposed of the gun and the bullets in a canal. Gary had told me that even if I didn't use it, there would be no refund. I also knew that if I had kept the gun, there was a possibility that I could still be tempted to use it on Hugh.

After about six weeks of taking the drugs, there was a significant change in my demeanour. I was no longer overconfident or making irrational decisions. The mental health unit that I attended had adjusted my medication as the weeks went on, and eventually Dr Jarrod told me that I had a condition known as "bipolar affective disorder" – otherwise known as manic depression.

I was confused by the term "manic depression", as I didn't feel depressed, but it was soon explained to me that the condition didn't mean that the person would necessarily suffer from depression. I read up on the condition, and recognized many of the symptoms that I had experienced.

While coming to terms with my condition, I was networking regularly and making some good contacts within the local business community. I was running my business successfully, and some of the professional businessmen and media consultants that I came in contact with were so impressed that I was put forward for a New Business of the Year award, which was run by the local newspaper.

Despite not winning my category at the lavish event, the whole experience had spurred me on to expand my business and fulfil my new dream of writing a book on project management.

PART NINE:

TURNING A CORNER

28

A NEW FOCUS

I settled into my self-employed role as a site management and health and safety trainer, and kept myself busy, developing some more management training courses. After watching a television programme that showed how unscrupulous builders and contractors were duping homeowners out of their life savings, I thought there would be a market for creating information and building guides for homeowners.

After preparing some sample chapters and a synopsis, I spent the next few months sending it out and in an effort to secure a publishing deal, but without any luck. I had plenty of letters from publishers to say 'Thanks but no, thanks,' but, in my usual manner I was determined to treat it as a project. Before long I decided to publish the book myself.

Having contacted a few friends and some networking colleagues, I had completed my book and sourced all the information that was needed to get it published. After just three months and lots of working into the night, it was ready. To see and feel the book in my hand filled me with pride and made me feel like I could do anything if I put my mind to it.

I didn't have any formal training in marketing, but having had my own business, it was something that came naturally to me. The book might have lacked a real professional publisher's feel, but nonetheless it was a good little book.

I sent the book to a handful of publishers with a covering letter saying that I would like to develop it further with an established publisher and the plan paid off.

I received an offer from a publisher, who told me that they liked the concept of my book but could I write an additional 15,000 words? I knew that it would be possible to expand on what I had already written – I had intentionally kept my little book to 10, 000 words because of budgetary constraints.

Within three weeks, I had met the publisher and signed a contract to deliver the manuscript to them within four months. I completed the book on time, and not long afterwards, it was published and on the shelves in high street bookshops up and down the country.

Seeing my name on a professionally published book was something that, until then, I had only dreamed of. Considering that I left school with no qualifications and that I am dyslexic, writing and getting a book published professionally, was no small feat.

Encouraged, I set about writing a much more comprehensive book on professional project management. Within the year I had secured another publishing deal, but I knew that the project was going to mean that I would have to halt my business activities for at least eight months.

I worked out my strategy for writing the book, taking the photographs and having the chapters reviewed by friends and family as I went along. Elizabeth was particularly helpful in reading my work and providing feedback, along with Edwin, who I met through the Chamber of Commerce. He had immediately taken a liking to me, and was only too happy to help me in any way he could, which was an enormous help to me later on.

Having wound down my business activities to virtually nothing, I started on the new book. I had some savings and had a few small investments, so I figured that I would be able to make ends meet until I was in a position to work again. I set out to write the book, and within two months I had written about a third of it.

My confidence was high, but I had been writing for about fourteen hours a day and it was starting to get to me. My social life before starting the book had been good, but for the two months that I had been writing, all I had seen were the four walls of the room in which I wrote. Apart from the odd shopping trip and an occasional visit to family members, I was pretty much locked in my flat.

After three months I was starting to doubt myself, and without the constant support that I had been used to when I was networking and running my business, I started to become depressed. I knew that there was one person who was capable of lifting my spirits and performance, and that was Edwin. I gave him a call and asked whether he would come round and give me some advice on an aspect of the book that was proving troublesome.

In reality I was not even halfway to completing the book and already I was ready to throw in the towel. Edwin arrived at the agreed time and we sat down and exchanged compliments.

'So, Rick, what seems to be the problem?' Edwin had spent much of his life in the Royal Navy. He was a softly spoken and had a wealth of experience behind him.

As I started to speak I broke down in tears.

'I can't do it, Edwin.' I had my head in my hands and my tears were falling to the floor so much that a small pool had started to form. 'I've racked my brain, and although I have my chapter headings I just don't know what to write.' I couldn't look up at Edwin, I felt ashamed for crying and just continued to look down at the floor as I sobbed.

Edwin knew that it would be best not to say anything and just let me compose myself. I could continue when I was ready to. Edwin knew that I was a proud man and wouldn't want to be made a fuss of, despite my desire for help.

'You must think I'm stupid, Edwin. I'm so sorry to ask you to come over, only to just embarrass myself.'

Again Edwin said nothing.

He had decided that when I sat up and looked at him – only then would he speak. Sure enough, I lifted my head and sat up, wiping the tears from my eyes.

'Could I have a cup of tea, please, Rick?' Edwin knew exactly how to handle the situation, and his calm demeanour was having the right effect on me. He knew that I would not have wanted a hand on my shoulder and the words, 'There, there, Rick, everything will be all right.' He knew that he had to re-motivate me, and from this point onwards, he decided that he would take a keener interest in the completion of the book.

'Oh, I'm so sorry, Edwin. I should have asked if you wanted a tea when you came in.'

I soon composed myself, and when I had made the tea I sat down and explained to Edwin my fear of not being able to deliver the book to the publisher. It wasn't a fear of any contractual failure, but more about failing to complete the book that just a few months earlier I had been so excited about writing.

'Rick, you are worn out. You need a break, that's all.'

Edwin spoke at length about what I had achieved over the past couple of years, and reminded me of my strongest asset, which was my determination to achieve my dreams. I had never been money-motivated, and my upbringing had taught me to be proud of my achievements and to believe in myself.

By the time Edwin left, I felt much more invigorated and decided to do as he'd suggested, and take a week off from writing.

It was summer, and although I had no work, I did live by the seaside, so I spent the next few days down on the beach, relaxing. I met up with Edwin during the week and received more words of encouragement.

I had shut myself away for too long while I concentrated on the book, so I made a point to spend more time with Matthew and Marie. Visiting the family, and doing normal things for just a few days, which soon brought me back to life.

I started back on the book, and to my surprise I had a new focus. I could think clearly again and, within two months, I was close to completing it.

I met Edwin on several occasions, having come to recognize when I needed the supportive and experienced words that only he could provide.

The book was ready to go and I delivered the manuscript to the publisher on time. I was disappointed to find out that it would take six months for the book to be completely finished, but I was also glad to be able to get back to doing some real work and topping up my bank account. I managed to get a couple of jobs building extensions for close friends, and by the time they were complete, I had more than replenished my bank account before the book came out.

Although I had seen the front cover of the book and had met the publishers on several occasions to agree on some of the details, I was so impressed by the completed book that it reduced me to tears of joy. In my eyes it was the culmination of all my hard work, and I knew it would help to propel my business and my career.

My tears were mainly born out of my sense of achievement. How I would have loved to show my parents what I had done. In all of my books, I always put in a statement to say, 'This book is written in memory of my mum and dad.'

29

MEDICAL RECORDS

Buoyed by the completion of my book, I decided to follow up on the news that the Freedom of Information Act had changed. I sent a letter to the organization responsible for releasing my mother's medical records.

After receiving a letter advising me that I was entitled to the information, but that it would take some time to compile, I continued to work and waited for the information to arrive.

Six weeks later, around the time the book was due to be released into the shops, I received a jiffy bag through the post. It was full of documents. I assumed at first that it was something from the publishers, and opened it without any preconceptions.

As soon as I saw the headed letter on the first page, I knew that it was the documentation that would give me some indication about my mother's mental condition when she was at the psychiatric unit. I sat down and read the pages and pages of handwritten records and information, which included notes by psychiatrists, doctors and nurses about my mother's time in 'the unit', as I knew it.

I was shocked to read that the voices that my mum heard in her head had been telling her to kill herself and her own children, and that it was all her fault that Hugh treated her so badly.

Within a very short space of time, I had the proof I needed to expose Hugh and what he had done to my mother. Whatever the doctors and nurses had done to extract the information and to get her to talk about her past, it was clear that she had been totally truthful about her life as a child and what she had endured.

It took me three hours to read the notes, and by the end of them I knew that I had to kill the man who had brought so much misery to my mother, particularly as I now had it in black and white that my mother had been sexually abused from the age of eleven until the age of sixteen. I knew that it would be futile in trying to take legal action as the victim – my mum – had long since died and could not give evidence.

I got into my car, after telling Stan what I was going to do, and drove over to Hugh's house with my heart pumping. I was going finally going to end Hugh's life once and for all. Stan tried to talk me out of going, but he knew that his words were futile.

When I arrived outside the house I was surprised to see that it had changed completely. It had been fitted with new windows and doors and had a new driveway and wrought-iron gates.

Across the road from Hugh's house was a man washing his car, so I decided to find out whether Hugh still lived there before knocking on the door.

'Excuse me,' I asked, 'does Hugh still live in the house across the road?'

'No, he's not there anymore,' said the man, with a quizzical look on his face. 'Did you know him?'

'Yes, I knew him. I knew him as "Granddad" until I found out he abused my mum when she was a child.'

'Are you the man who visited Hugh some years before, to collect some photographs?'

'Yes, that's me, and if I'm reading this right Hugh is dead, yeah?'

'That's right. He died about eighteen months ago, of a heart attack at home.'

'Well,' I said in a happy tone, 'that's going to save me a job then, I'd just come round to kill him.'

The man looked at me in astonishment.

'Pardon, did I hear you correctly?'

'You sure did,' I said with a smile on my face, 'I've just received the proof I needed that he was a monster towards my mum.'

'We had heard over the years that he was a paedophile, and everyone was wary of him.' The man looked me straight in the eye. 'Was it you who put the letters through the doors of everyone in the street?'

'It was indeed,' I said. 'I couldn't have it on my conscience if he managed to touch any children.' Then I thanked the man and got back into my car.

As I drove away, I reflected on something I'd done about eighteen months earlier. I had been driving past the end of Hugh's road when I happened to see Hugh walking his dog. I pulled over and decided to let Hugh know that he was still being watched.

'Hugh!' I shouted from my car window.

As the old man looked over, I hid my face slightly behind the pillar of the car door.

Hugh walked over and right up to the car door.

'Hello Granddad. Remember me, you old bastard?' My voice was cold and harsh and full of hatred.

Hugh turned and shuffled off with his dog in tow.

I went round the block and waited about twenty yards up the road from Hugh's front gate.

As Hugh walked up the road as fast as his old legs would take him, he was looking round to see whether I was following him. As he approached his gate I put my foot on the accelerator and screeched down the road, pulling up at the gate just as Hugh was opening it. I was glad to see that the fear on Hugh's face was real and that his face had drained of blood.

'Don't forget, you old bastard: I am behind you wherever you go, and I will fucking haunt you.'

I drove off feeling exhilarated, but strangely shaken. I was not a violent man but when it came to Hugh, a different side of me came out.

One thing that always puzzled me about that chance meeting with Hugh was that I had expected a knock on the door from the police. I had breached the terms of the court order that was placed on me by Hugh's solicitor to keep away from Hugh's house by half a mile.

So if what the man had said was true, which I had no reason to believe it wasn't, then Hugh had died at about the same time.

'Is it possible?' I asked myself. 'Did that chance meeting frighten Hugh so much that he had a heart attack?'

I was never going to know the answer to that question, but my gut feeling told me what I wanted to believe.

30

RELEASE

I now had my new book and was going to use it to my advantage. Edwin had suggested that I should become a technical author, and use my skills to write safety manuals and other documentation for large organisations.

I signed up with a few agencies, and within a couple of weeks I was receiving phone calls from recruitment consultants wanting to speak to me about positions that they had on offer and thought would be suitable.

I secured a job working for a large transport organization, writing health and safety manuals and guidance documents. I thoroughly enjoyed the work and was earning extremely good money. Being part of a big team gave the work so much more of a purpose and I soon realised how lonely I had been when writing my own material by myself. Interacting with people in an environment where I had everything I needed at my disposal was very satisfying.

It had been a long time since I had felt this happy. I moved from my seaside town to London, and into a house share with five Polish people, two Hungarians, a French woman and a Turkish man. At the age of 46, I felt a little old to be sharing a house, but that feeling soon wore off.

The housemates made me feel welcome. When they found out I was a published author, they were very impressed, which made me feel very humble although I was proud of my achievements.

Ever since Mum and Dad had died, I maintained contact with Nan and Jenny, and our relationship became very strong and loving.

Although Nan was approaching eighty-one, she was funny, bright and always smiling, despite some very severe ailments that crippled her with chronic pain. Her daughter, Jenny, had become a full-time carer when Nan had been diagnosed.

Nan knew that Mum had spent time in and out of psychiatric units during her life, but she had never fully known the reasons behind it. Although they had developed a mother-daughter relationship, it had come too late in Mum's life for her to be able to open up to her real mother. Mum did not want to tell her what had happened to her, as she understood why she had been given up for adoption and she didn't want Nan to feel any unnecessary guilt.

Although Nan had other grandchildren, she always made me feel special. Well at least that's how I felt, and I was sure she felt the same way too. There's only a two year difference between Jenny and me, so we've always had a natural easy banter.

My siblings and I had never really discussed what had happened to our Mum. We all dealt with it in our own ways, although I had never let it far from my mind. It was only when I began attending AA meetings that I started to exorcise it from my mind, and make sense of what happened.

Of all of the things that I had done to Hugh over the years, I never felt remorseful and only wished that I had done more to hurt him. I did see, however, in hindsight, that I had not allowed myself to forgive or forget, and that I had in some ways been persecuting not just Hugh, but myself as well. It wasn't good for me to be so obsessed with violence and revenge, and it certainly wasn't good for my wife and kids to see me deteriorate to an alcoholic. I knew I could turn things round with the help of AA.

During the AA meetings I recounted that the pain I felt when I found out what my mother had suffered at the hands of Hugh was like having my heart ripped out. But as the meetings went on, and I wrote down my thoughts, I told my fellow AA members that I felt as though I was growing a new heart.

I had led a very varied life, my daughter, Marie, suggested to me that I should write a book about it. Marie in particular had always wanted me to tell her stories about where I had been and what I had done and she took everything in.

I had done and seen things in life that most people would not have had the opportunity to do, or in many cases would not have wanted to experience.

I remember asking Marie, 'But why would people want to hear my story?'

'Come on, Dad,' she said, 'you have funny stories, sad stories, happy stories, and you have done things that I'm sure people would love to hear about.'

I consider my life to have been one of happiness as a child and, when it came to raising children of my own as a young father, it had been demanding and difficult. Although I had enjoyed seeing my children grow, from the time of my parents' deaths within seventeen months of each other, my life had become marred by mental anguish, drink, recovery and reconciliation.

'Why would you *not* want to tell people your story, Dad?' Marie went on, 'Everyone loves it when you tell them all the things you have done, whether they were good or bad.'

Marie was right. When I got into my stride, telling people about something that I had done, seen, heard or built, they were always keen to hear more. I decided to take my daughter's advice, and started work on a story that would be hard-hitting and emotional, but, I hoped, at the same time warm and touching.

I worked out my plan, and contacted an established ghost-writer. We agreed on how much it would cost and roughly how many sessions would be required. We met in Bristol where she lived, meeting at a hotel where she had booked an interview room to start work on the book.

'Okay, Rick, how I work is that I'll tape the meetings and ask you a series of questions about your life, and after that I'll write it up into chapters.' The ghost-writer was very clear about how things would proceed, and I was excited and ready to get going.

The first session started and before very long I was in floods of tears. It was clear to the ghost-writer that my mother had been the one who dominated the majority of my recollections, both during her lifetime and afterwards.

We had several more sessions together, but it did not generate many chapters, and eventually I could not afford to keep going to Bristol. The ghost-writer then had other commitments and after a few months, the project fizzled out.

I shelved the project, but I knew that at some point later on, when I was more able to discuss things, I would develop it further. I am not a person to start a project without completing it and I was keen to finish the book, the subject of which was how the actions of one man could taint the life of so many people. I decided that I would call it *If You Dare Tell*.

And there my story ends. Yes, this is me, Rick, with a few words directly from me to you, my reader.

Writing *If You Dare Tell* has been an incredible roller coaster of a ride. I never considered myself capable of writing such a story, and although I am very driven and possess the discipline to complete the book, it has only been possible with the assistance of some close and special people.

My Nan is still alive, and although she is elderly she has a young mind and makes me laugh so much. Jenny and I are very close, although we do not see each other as often as I'd like.

My brothers and sister have supported me in everything I have ever done, and when I was at my lowest ebb, they were the ones who helped pull me through. Never once did they walk away from me, even though I felt that I didn't deserve such loyalty.

Anne and I remain the best of friends. We spend Christmases and special occasions together, with our two children, Matthew and Marie, and our grandson Reece. It is safe to say that we are a very happy family unit.

I continue to take medication for bipolar affective disorder, and I'm glad to say that it works.

If I have one message that I'd like to impart it is that people should try to be less vengeful and to try more to forgive. I can't forgive, but as time goes on I feel much more at ease about what happened to the two people who made me the man who I am today, my mum and dad.